# The Best
# Grill Pan
# Cookbook Ever

# The Best
# Grill Pan
# Cookbook Ever

## Marge Poore

A John Boswell Associates/King Hill Productions Book

HarperCollins*Publishers*

HarperCollins books may be purchased for educational, business, or sales promotional use. For information please write: Special Markets Department, HarperCollins Publishers, Inc., 10 East 53rd Street, New York, NY 10022.

FIRST EDITION

Design: *Barbara Cohen Aronica*
Index: *Maro Riofrancos*

ISBN 0-06-018798-0

99   00   01   02   03   HC   10   9   8   7   6   5   4   3   2   1

# *Contents*

# Introduction

## *Stove-Top Grill Pans Are Great!*

Being able to grill anytime, without the bother of setting up outdoors or the risk of a turn in the weather, is reason enough to own one of the wonderful new stove-top grill pans that have recently skyrocketed in popularity. In addition, most of the new pans have large cooking surfaces and nonstick finishes, although some new grill pans do require seasoning before first-time use. All of the manufacturers here include instructions for using their pans, so just follow their advice and your pan will give you great results and lots of pleasure for a long time.

Grilling in the kitchen is easy and quick. There is very little smoke or mess, because very little fat is used, and the pans have ridges that hold the food away from any fat that does drip into the pan. The pans work equally well on gas or electric stove tops, and they can also go into the oven. There are many models and sizes and quite a range of prices to choose from when shopping for a grill pan. Some are round and some are square or oblong. Some have handles, some do not, and some have griddles on the bottom surface. Oblong models can be used on two burners at once, increasing the cooking surface. Whichever style you choose, you'll quickly realize how simple it is to give that outdoor charred flavor and distinctive grill-marked look to foods cooked on a stove-top grill pan. The current rage for grilled foods has certainly prompted manufacturers to design excellent grill pans for home use.

The seven chapters in this book cover all kinds of foods that are grill-friendly. They contain over 150 recipes that demonstrate how convenient and easy it is to achieve distinctive grill marks and slightly smoky flavors while cooking indoors, anytime, on a stove-top grill pan. This is healthy, low-fat cooking that encourages a diet of lean meats, fish, poultry, and fresh seasonal vegetables. Besides making foods taste and look wonderful, the grill pan also offers easy cleanup. So, put your grill pan to work, and enjoy the recipes in this book, which have been created especially for this kind of cooking.

# About Makes and Models of Stove-Top Grill Pans

A walk through a well-stocked cookware store or a glance through a cook's catalog will show you that grill pans are in high demand. Ridged stove-top grill pans and skillet grill pans from any number of manufacturers offer different sizes, shapes, and materials. The prices are all over the map, with most models deeply discounted if you look in the right stores and catalogs. Whether square, round, oblong, single- or double-burner style, there's a grill pan to fit every cook's needs, preference, and budget. The basic design of any stove-top grill pan does not vary greatly: it has shallow or minimal sides and ridged raised grills on the bottom that conduct the heat and create the distinctive grill marks. When foods are cooked this way, flavors are maximized and calories minimized, because the raised ridges, which not only make foods brown better, also lock in flavors and give foods a caramelized smoky taste, while the fat drips away into the grooves and a lower trough that usually runs around the bottom rim of the pan.

Following are some of the manufacturers who currently offer stove-top grill pans. Since this product is so popular, newer makes and models may already be on the market when this book comes out. All of the grill pans listed here perform well on gas or electric stovetops, but are not recommended for use on flat-surface induction-type stovetops.

### Calphalon

This well-known and popular brand of high-quality, heavy-duty cookware has four lines of stove-top grill pans. There are three high-end lines offered by Calphalon, which are the Original, the Professional, and the Commercial Nonstick. The Original are hard, anodized-surface pans with a raised outside edge and steel handles. They are available in 11-inch square and 12-inch round sizes. Both are priced at $75. The Professional line features heavier anodized pans with a raised outside edge and steel handles, which are also available in 11-inch square and 12-inch round sizes. Both are priced at $85. The Commercial Nonstick line is the newest heavy-duty and toughest of the Calphalon grill pans on the market. This new line also has a raised outside edge and steel handles and is available in 11-inch square and 12-inch round sizes. Both are priced at $95.

Calphalon's most moderately priced line is their Pots&Pans label. It is a lighter-weight pan with a nonstick surface, raised outside edge, and a comfortable, black, heat-free handle. This pan is a roomy 13-inch round, which heats quickly but less evenly than the heavier models. Price: $40.

## Chef's Design

There are two sizes offered by this manufacturer. A double-burner, reversible range-top grill is 10 by 20 inches, big enough to use on two burners at the same time. The pan is ridged on one side for grilling and smooth on the other for use as a griddle. A square single-burner reversible range-top grill is 10 by 10 inches. Both sizes are heavy-gauge cast aluminum, with no handle and only a slightly raised outside edge. Extra care must be taken to prevent getting burned when moving the hot pan. Price is $49 for the double, $39 for the single.

## All-Clad

Premier quality cookware with an excellent reputation. Two heavy-duty grill pans are available: an 11-inch square and the new 12-inch round. Both pans feature a hard, anodized, nonstick ridged surface with a raised outside edge and a handle that stays cool. These pans conduct heat evenly to produce excellent results and can be used in a 400 degree F. oven. The nonstick finish is guaranteed for life and is very easy to clean. Price $120.

## Circulon

Medium-weight nonstick grill pans with heat-resistant plastic handles. The hard anodized aluminum heats fast and is very durable. Prices range greatly depending upon size. A convenient 8-inch single serving round pan is $20; a 12-inch round, $60; and a 14-inch round, $80.

## Analon

Two sizes are offered by Analon: a small pan that is useful when cooking for one or two, and a large one for entertaining or family use. Both sizes have a lifetime guarantee and feature a hard-anodized nonstick surface that conducts heat quickly and evenly. Both have stainless steel stay-cool handles. The pans are oven-safe to 500 degrees F. A 9½-inch square pan costs $60; a 14-inch round grill pan costs $110.

## LeCreuset

Classic cookware made in France, known for its durability, good looks, and high quality. Made of heavy cast iron, which heats quickly and evenly and can stand the hottest oven temperatures. LeCreuset offers an oblong skillet grill, 12½ by 9 inches; price: $100. Two round skillet grills, 10-inch and 12-inch; prices: $100 and $110, respectively. One 10-inch square skillet grill; price: $100. All of the skillet grills have handles, enameled outside finish, and a higher outside edge than most other makes. There are also two reversible heavy flat black cast-iron pans with narrow close-set grids that give excellent professional-looking grill marks. The double-burner 9 by 18-inch pan costs $100, and the single-burner 10 by 10-inch pan costs $75.

## Wearever

Lightweight, affordable 12-inch round Health Grill skillet with handle and ridged Maxalon nonstick interior, which carries a 10-year limited warranty; price: $20.

## Look

High-end quality cookware made in Iceland. There is one grill pan in the line. A square 10½-inch pan gives great cooking performance. The bakelite handle stays cool on the stove. The easy-to-clean pan is nonstick inside and out and ovenproof to 500 degrees F. Advance technique casting of aluminum over a double layer of Quattrex nonstick coating makes the pan heat rapidly and evenly; price: $72.50. Accessory high dome cover of Pyrex, which doubles as a serving dish, is available at $30.

## Farberware

There are three different sizes of lightweight, moderately priced grill pans in this line. Both 9½-inch and 12-inch round grill pans have nonstick surfaces. Price for each: $30. Farberware also makes an 11-inch square grill pan priced at $32.

## Nordic Ware

Reversible double-burner 19 by 11-inch rectangular pan of gray cast aluminum that won't rust or warp. Coated with Nordic Ware's nonstick finish with a ridged grill on one side and a smooth griddle surface on the other; price: $30.

## Wagner's

Original 1891 fat-free heavy cast-iron ridged skillet that heats evenly and gets very hot. High oven heat is okay. Mama Wagner's seasoning instructions, cleaning tips, and secrets come with the skillet. With good care and proper seasoning, it will last a lifetime. An 11½-inch round ridged skillet is priced at $20.

- Nonstick cooking spray, such as Pam, can be used safely on some pan surfaces. Follow the manufacturers' instructions for your particular pan. If using cooking spray, spray onto a cool pan. Then preheat the pan. The reason to be cautious about cooking spray is that it can build up on the pan surface and, in time, it may cause the pan to lose its nonstick quality. Brushing the food lightly with vegetable oil before grilling is probably the best way to prevent foods from sticking, and also aids in better browning and helps to seal in moisture.
- To achieve grill marks in a distinctive cross-hatch pattern on foods like steaks, burgers, toasted breads, etc., cook the food until parallel grill marks appear, then rotate the food 90 degrees for a second set of marks.
- For best stove-top grilling results and for easier handling, foods should be less than 1½ inches thick. Thicker, larger pieces cook best by being first seared on the grill pan and then transferred to a hot oven to finish cooking.

In a short time, you will learn how easy it is to get great results from your grill pan by using the recipes in this book, and in a little more time, you will be creating ideas of your own. Indoor grilling will probably become second nature, and the grill pan will be one of your most important pieces of kitchen equipment.

## Chapter One
# Sizzling Starters

Appetizers set the mood for many occasions. Sometimes they're a light snack to keep us going between meals; often they're a convivial overture before the main event. Whenever you're considering what appetizers to serve, check the ideas in this chapter. You'll find plenty of ways to use grill pans to prepare hot hors d'oeuvres that are served right off the grill. Much of the work for the recipes in this chapter can be done ahead, and the final grilling is quick, thanks to the ease of using a grill pan.

Among the quick-to-fix bites to serve with cocktails are Cocktail Time Shrimp on Picks, Crab Quesadillas, and Toasted Pita Wedges with Herbed Goat Cheese. There are also informal foods, such as Polish Kielbasa Sausage Snacks and Beef Teriyaki on a Stick, which make ideal snacks for casual occasions. Other recipes—Mushroom Caps Stuffed with Ham, Grilled Shrimp with Romesco Sauce, and Turkey Nuggets with Grilled Red Onion Dipping Sauce among them—are especially suited for buffet parties.

# Bruschetta with Red Bell Pepper, Scallions, and Feta Cheese

*Pile a fresh red bell pepper topping on grilled French bread for a hearty appetizer or serve the bruschetta with pasta salad for a light lunch.*

*Makes 6 servings*

---

3 tablespoons olive oil
1 red bell pepper, cut into ¼-inch dice
3 scallions, chopped
2 garlic cloves, finely chopped
1 teaspoon fresh lemon juice

4 ounces crumbled feta cheese
3 or 4 grinds of pepper
12 slices of French bread, cut ½ inch thick

---

**1.** In a medium nonstick skillet, heat 1 tablespoon of the olive oil over medium heat. Add the bell pepper, scallions, and garlic and cook, stirring, until barely tender, 2 to 3 minutes. Transfer to a medium bowl and let cool 5 minutes. Add the lemon juice, feta cheese, and pepper. Toss gently. Set the topping aside.

**2.** Brush both sides of the bread lightly with the remaining 2 tablespoons of olive oil. Heat a grill pan over medium heat until hot enough to make a few drops of water sizzle. Lay the bread on the pan and grill both sides until lightly toasted and marked from the grill, 3 to 4 minutes total. Pile a portion of the topping on each bread slice and arrange on a platter. Serve warm or at room temperature.

# Catalan Tomato Toast

*Marimar Torres, president of Torres Wines North America, showed me how to make pan con tomate, classic tomato toasts from the Catalonian region of Spain, at a luncheon in her beautiful California winery. This very simple seasonal treat is best when vine-ripened tomatoes are available. The grill pan toasts the bread quickly, adding appealing grill marks, so you can enjoy these on a moment's notice.*

*Makes 4 servings*

---

8 large slices of good country bread or sourdough bread, cut ½ inch thick
3 tablespoons extra-virgin olive oil
2 large garlic cloves, peeled and halved crosswise

2 large vine-ripened tomatoes, halved crosswise
Salt and freshly ground pepper

---

**1.** Brush both sides of the bread lightly with 1 tablespoon of the olive oil. Heat a grill pan over medium heat until hot enough to make a few drops of water sizzle. Toast the bread, in batches if necessary, until marked from the grill on both sides, 3 to 4 minutes.

**2.** Rub 1 side of each bread slice with the cut sides of the garlic halves. With half of a tomato cupped in your hand, "grate" the tomato half over 2 slices of grilled bread. Squeeze the tomato so that the juice and some of the pulp get spread on the bread. Repeat with the remaining 6 slices of bread.

**3.** Drizzle the remaining 2 tablespoons of olive oil over the tomato toast. Season with salt and pepper to taste. Serve at once.

# Cheese and Salsa Quesadillas

*Whenever a quick and sure-to-please appetizer is needed, easy cheese quesadillas are my answer. Toasting them on a grill pan makes them taste even better and look more attractive with the stamp of the grids on the tortillas.*

*Makes 4 servings*

---

4 (7-inch) flour tortillas
¼ cup prepared red salsa
1 cup shredded Cheddar or Monterey
   Jack cheese (about 4 ounces)

2 teaspoons vegetable oil

---

**1.** Heat a grill pan over medium-high heat until hot enough to make a few drops of water sizzle. Quickly warm the tortillas on the grill, turning 2 or 3 times, until soft and pliable, about 15 seconds on each side.

**2.** Lay the warm tortillas out flat and spread 1 tablespoon of salsa over each. Put ¼ cup of cheese on half the surface of each tortilla and fold over to form a semicircle. Brush each tortilla lightly with vegetable oil.

**3.** Lay the quesadillas on the hot grill pan. Toast, turning once with a wide spatula, until the quesadillas are browned on both sides and the cheese is melted, 2 to 3 minutes. Cut into wedges and serve hot.

# Zucchini, Jalapeño, and Cheese Quesadillas

*Shredded fresh zucchini and bits of zippy jalapeño enclosed in flour tortillas make an easy finger snack that's quick to assemble and easy to toast on the grill pan.*

*Makes 16 pieces*

---

2 medium zucchini, shredded
2 fresh jalapeño peppers, seeded and
  minced
2 scallions, chopped
¼ teaspoon salt

2 tablespoons vegetable oil or olive oil
2½ tablespoons butter, at room
  temperature
8 (7- or 8-inch) flour tortillas
1 cup shredded Monterey Jack cheese

---

**1.** Put the zucchini, jalapeños, scallions, and salt in a medium bowl. Toss to mix. In a medium skillet, heat the oil over medium-high heat. Add the zucchini mixture and sauté, stirring often, until the zucchini is bright green at the edges and barely tender, 2 to 3 minutes. Remove from the heat.

**2.** Brush the soft butter lightly on both sides of the tortillas. Spoon one-fourth of the zucchini mixture onto each of 4 tortillas. Spread to within ½ inch of the edges. Sprinkle ¼ cup of the cheese over the zucchini and top with another tortilla. Press the quesadillas lightly with the palm of your hand to partially seal.

**3.** Heat a grill pan over medium heat until hot enough to make a few drops of water sizzle. Lay 1 or 2 quesadillas on the hot pan and toast until crispy, with brown grill marks on the bottom, 3 to 4 minutes. Using a wide spatula, carefully flip over and toast the second side until the tortilla is crisp and brown and the cheese is melted, 2 to 3 minutes. Repeat with the remaining quesadillas. Cut the quesadillas into quarters and arrange on a serving plate. Serve while warm and crisp.

---

# Corn Tortilla Quesadillas with Brie and Jalapeños

*Soft corn tortillas with melted Brie cheese and strips of fresh jalapeño peppers served hot from the grill pan are slightly chewy on the outside, warm and creamy on the inside—with just a little crunch from the peppers. It's a great combination. Here the quesadillas are cut into wedges for easy finger food.*

*Makes 16 pieces*

---

8 (6- or 7-inch) corn tortillas
1 (6-ounce) container of spreadable Brie cheese

4 large fresh jalapeño peppers, seeded and cut into ¼-inch strips
4 teaspoons vegetable oil

---

**1.** Lay out 2 corn tortillas on a flat surface. Spread a thin layer of the Brie over each tortilla to within ½ inch of the edges. Arrange 8 to 10 jalapeño strips on the surface of 1 of the tortillas. Lay the other tortilla, cheese side down, over the jalapeño strips to form a sandwich. Repeat with the remaining jalapeños and tortillas. Brush the tops of the quesadillas lightly with 2 teaspoons of the vegetable oil.

**2.** Heat a grill pan over medium heat until hot enough to make a few drops of water sizzle. Using a wide spatula, flip the quesadillas onto the heated pan, oiled sides down, and toast until the tortillas have light brown grill marks on the bottom, 3 to 4 minutes. Before turning the quesadillas over, brush the tops lightly with the remaining 2 teaspoons of oil. Using the spatula, carefully turn the quesadillas over. Toast until the cheese is melted and the second side of the tortillas is marked with light brown grill marks, about 3 minutes.

**3.** Transfer the quesadillas to a cutting board. With a large chef's knife, cut straight down to divide the quesadillas in half. Repeat in the opposite direction to cut into 4 equal pieces. Serve hot.

# Grilled Corn Cakes with Mushroom Ragout

*Stove-top grilling produces tender cornmeal cakes with a delicate light brown crust. The mushroom topping can be prepared ahead and reheated just before serving. This recipe makes a satisfying first course. For a great light meal, add a salad.*

*Makes 4 servings*

---

1 cup yellow cornmeal
⅓ cup grated Parmesan or Romano cheese
1 tablespoon butter
½ teaspoon salt
2 tablespoons olive oil
1 small onion, thinly sliced

1 pound mushrooms, thinly sliced
¼ cup dry vermouth or white wine
1 tablespoon Worcestershire sauce
1 tablespoon tomato paste
⅛ teaspoon freshly ground pepper
1 tablespoon chopped parsley

---

**1.** Butter an 8-inch-square pan. In a heavy medium saucepan, bring 3 cups of water to a boil over high heat. Reduce the heat to medium-low. Gradually add the cornmeal, whisking constantly to prevent lumps. Cook until the cornmeal is thick and smooth and starts to leave a film on the bottom of the pan, 12 to 15 minutes. Stir in the cheese, butter, and salt. Immediately spread the hot cornmeal evenly in the buttered pan. Set aside to cool and set for 1 hour, or cover and refrigerate overnight. Let the cornmeal return to room temperature before grilling.

**2.** In a large skillet, heat the olive oil over medium-high heat. Add the onion and cook until softened and translucent, 2 to 3 minutes. Add the mushrooms and cook, stirring until the juices are almost evaporated, 4 to 5 minutes. Stir in the vermouth, Worcestershire, and tomato paste. Cover, reduce the heat to low, and simmer for

5 minutes. Season with the pepper. Remove the mushroom ragout from the heat and cover to keep warm.

**3.** Cut the cornmeal into 4 squares, then cut each square diagonally in half to make 2 triangles each. Coat a grill pan with nonstick cooking spray, then heat over medium heat until hot enough to make a few drops of water sizzle. Put the cornmeal triangles on the hot pan, smooth side down, and cook until lightly browned on the bottom, 3 to 4 minutes. Turn over and cook 1 to 2 minutes on the second side to heat through.

**4.** To serve, put 2 corn cakes on each of 4 plates and spoon the mushroom ragout on top. Garnish with the chopped parsley and serve.

# Toasted Pita Triangles with Hummus

*The Middle Eastern chickpea puree called hummus is popular both as a spread and as a dip. Here I serve it with toasted pita bread straight from the grill pan. Add crisp sliced cucumbers and a bowl of olives for an easy and enticing appetizer.*

*Makes 4 servings*

---

1 (15-ounce) can chickpeas (garbanzo beans), drained and rinsed
3 garlic cloves, crushed through a press
¼ cup fresh lemon juice
3 tablespoons olive oil
2 tablespoons tahini (Middle Eastern sesame paste)

1 teaspoon paprika
½ teaspoon ground cumin
Salt and freshly ground pepper
1½ teaspoons chopped parsley
6 (7-inch) pita breads, cut into triangles

---

**1.** In a food processor, combine the chickpeas, garlic, lemon juice, 2 tablespoons of the olive oil, the tahini, paprika, cumin, and 1 tablespoon of water. Puree until smooth. If the hummus is too thick to be spreadable, add more water ½ teaspoon at a time. Season to taste with salt and pepper. Transfer to a serving bowl. Sprinkle the parsley on top. If making ahead, cover and refrigerate for up to 1 day.

**2.** Brush the pita triangles lightly with the remaining 1 tablespoon of olive oil on both sides. Heat a grill pan over medium heat until hot enough to make a few drops of water sizzle. Put the pita triangles on the hot grill pan in batches as necessary. Toast, turning, until lightly marked from the grill and crisp, 1 to 2 minutes on each side.

**3.** Put the pita triangles in a napkin-lined basket and serve warm with the hummus.

# Toasted Pita Wedges with Herbed Goat Cheese

*Here's another way to enjoy pita breads toasted on the grill pan—with goat cheese blended with chives and fresh herbs. Choose a mild, fresh goat cheese, such as Coach Farm or Montrachet.*

*Makes 4 servings*

---

4 ounces mild white goat cheese (chèvre), at room temperature

3 ounces cream cheese, at room temperature

2 tablespoons chopped fresh dill

2 tablespoons chopped flat-leaf parsley

1 tablespoon chopped chives

¼ teaspoon freshly ground pepper

Salt (optional)

6 (7-inch) whole wheat or plain pita breads

2 teaspoons olive oil

---

**1.** In a food processor, combine the goat cheese, cream cheese, dill, parsley, chives, and pepper. Puree until smooth and blended. Taste and season with salt if desired. Transfer the spread to a small serving bowl.

**2.** Brush the pita breads on both sides with the olive oil. Cut the pitas into quarters. Heat a grill pan over medium heat until hot enough to make a few drops of water sizzle. Put the pita quarters on the pan and toast, turning, until lightly marked from the grill, 1 to 2 minutes on each side. Serve warm or at room temperature in a basket, with the herbed cheese spread on the side.

# Mushroom Caps Stuffed with Ham

*An easy two-step method for grilling and stuffing mushroom caps creates delicious finger food to pass at a party. For convenience, the stuffing can be prepared in advance.*

*Makes 24*

---

½ cup finely chopped smoked ham (about 2½ ounces)

½ cup finely shredded sharp cheddar cheese

¼ cup chopped black olives

1 scallion, finely chopped

2 teaspoons mayonnaise

24 medium white mushrooms (about 1½ inches across)

2 tablespoons olive oil

---

**1.** In a medium bowl, combine the ham, cheese, olives, scallion, and mayonnaise. Mix together until blended. Set the filling aside. If made ahead, cover and refrigerate.

**2.** Remove the mushroom stems. Clean the caps by brushing or wiping them with a damp paper towel. Rub the mushrooms all over with olive oil. Heat a grill pan over medium heat until hot enough to make a few drops of water sizzle.

**3.** Put the mushrooms, cup side down, on the hot pan. Cook until brown grill marks appear around the edges, 3 to 4 minutes. Turn the mushrooms over and cook until juices appear in the cups, 2 to 3 minutes. Pour whatever you can of these juices into the ham filling and set the grilled mushrooms on a plate.

**4.** Fill each cap with about 1 teaspoon of the ham filling. Return the stuffed mushrooms to the grill pan, filled sides up. Cover loosely with foil and cook until the cheese melts, 1 to 2 minutes. Serve hot.

# Grilled Zucchini with Basil and Lemon

*Everyone loves munching on fried zucchini, though the fat is not always wel-
come. Grilling is a better, lighter way of enjoying the amazingly adaptable,
always available vegetable.*

*Makes 4 servings*

---

3 medium zucchini (about 1 pound)  
1 tablespoon olive oil  
¼ teaspoon salt  

3 or 4 grinds of pepper  
2 tablespoons fresh lemon juice  
1 tablespoon slivered fresh basil  

---

**1.** Rinse the zucchini and pat dry. Trim off the ends. Cut on the diagonal into oval
slices ¼ inch thick. Use a fairly wide angle so the slices are as large as possible. Put
them into a medium bowl. Add the olive oil, salt, and pepper and toss to coat.

**2.** Heat a grill pan over medium heat until hot enough to make a few drops of water
sizzle. Lay the zucchini slices on the pan and cook until grill marks appear on the
bottom, 2 to 3 minutes. Turn over and cook until crisp-tender and still bright green
around the edges, 1 to 2 minutes.

**3.** Arrange the zucchini pieces in overlapping rows on a serving plate. Shortly before
serving, drizzle with the lemon juice and scatter the basil on top. Serve warm or at
room temperature.

# Crab and Avocado Toasts

*Crisp whole wheat toasts topped with a light crab and avocado salad make a fine hors d'oeuvre or light lunch. These go beautifully with a glass of chilled Sauvignon Blanc. If you have a choice, use rough-skinned Hass avocados. To be ripe, they should have the softness of a peach.*

*Makes 32 pieces*

---

½ pound fresh crabmeat
3 tablespoons mayonnaise
1 tablespoon fresh lime juice
4 or 5 dashes of Tabasco or other hot
  sauce
¼ teaspoon salt

2 ripe avocados, coarsely chopped
8 slices of whole wheat bread
1½ tablespoons unsalted butter, at room
  temperature
Chopped parsley

---

**1.** Pick over the crab to remove any bits of shell or cartilage. In a medium bowl, combine the mayonnaise, lime juice, Tabasco, and salt. Blend well. Add the crab and avocado and mix gently. Cover and refrigerate.

**2.** Toast the bread, then butter 1 side of each toasted bread slice. Heat a grill pan over medium heat until hot enough to make a few drops of water sizzle. Put the bread on the heated grill, buttered sides down. Grill until brown grill marks appear, 2 to 3 minutes. Turn the bread over and grill the second side until lightly browned, 2 to 3 minutes longer.

**3.** Top the toasts with the crab-avocado salad. Garnish with the parsley and cut into quarters. Serve at once.

# Crab Quesadillas

*Crab and cheese layered on tortillas make memorable quesadillas. Crisp up the tortillas on a grill pan for great-looking and great-tasting appetizers.*

*Makes 24 pieces*

---

8 (8-inch) flour tortillas
½ cup prepared Mexican green salsa
¾ cup shredded Monterey Jack cheese
   (about 4 ounces)

1 (6-ounce) can crabmeat
¼ cup vegetable oil

---

**1.** Lay out 4 of the tortillas on a flat work surface. Spread 2 tablespoons green salsa over 1 side of each tortilla to within ½ inch of the edges. Cover each with 3 tablespoons cheese and 2 to 3 tablespoons crabmeat. Lay the remaining 4 tortillas on top and brush the surface of the tortillas lightly with oil.

**2.** Heat a grill pan over medium heat until hot enough to make a few drops of water sizzle. Lay 1 quesadilla, oiled side down, on the hot pan and toast until crisp and light brown on the bottom, 2 to 3 minutes. With a wide spatula, turn over and grill 2 minutes longer. Repeat with the remaining 3 quesadillas. Let stand 1 to 2 minutes. Cut each quesadilla into 6 wedges and serve.

# Crispy Crab Cakes

*Fresh crab makes the very best crab cakes, so I recommend using fresh whenever possible, but good-quality canned crabmeat also works for this recipe. These crab cakes are easy to make and become crisp and brown when cooked on a stove-top grill pan.*

*Makes about 12 (2-inch) crab cakes*

---

½ pound cooked fresh or canned
  crabmeat
2 scallions, minced
½ cup fine dry bread crumbs
1 egg, lightly beaten

1 teaspoon Worcestershire sauce
2 or 3 drops Tabasco sauce
2 tablespoons vegetable oil
Mayonnaise or seafood cocktail sauce

---

**1.** In a medium bowl, combine the crabmeat, scallions, crumbs, egg, Worcestershire, and Tabasco. Spread 1 tablespoon of the oil on a baking sheet. With your hands, form the crab mixture into 2-inch cakes, and put the crab cakes on the oiled baking sheet. With your fingers, dab the remaining 1 tablespoon of the oil on the surface of the crab cakes. Cover and refrigerate for 30 minutes, or until ready to cook.

**2.** Heat a grill pan over medium heat until hot enough to make a few drops of water sizzle. Put the crab cakes on the heated pan, and cook until crisp and brown on the bottom, about 4 minutes. Turn the cakes over, and cook the second side for 2 to 3 minutes. Serve hot with mayonnaise or cocktail sauce.

# Cocktail Time Shrimp on Picks

*Here's a no-panic appetizer using ready-to-cook frozen shrimp, which are available in most supermarket frozen foods sections. The shrimp are individually frozen, allowing you to remove exactly the amount you need from the package, while keeping the rest frozen. This recipe calls for a 12-ounce package, which contains about 40 frozen, cleaned, and deveined shrimp with their tails intact. Just thaw and grill. Skewer the shrimp with fancy little cocktail toothpicks to serve with drinks. It's fun to add a martini-style olive or onion to the picks with the shrimp.*

*Makes about 10 appetizer servings*

---

1 (12-ounce) package frozen, cleaned,
   ready-to-cook shrimp
1 large garlic clove, finely chopped
1 teaspoon soy sauce

1 tablespoon olive oil
Cocktail onions or olives (optional)
Parsley sprigs and lemon wedges

---

**1.** Thaw the shrimp, following the directions on the package. Drain well, and put in a glass baking dish. Pat with paper towels to remove excess moisture. Add the garlic, soy, and olive oil. Toss the shrimp to coat with the marinade, and let stand for about 20 minutes. Heat a grill pan over medium heat until hot enough to make a few drops of water sizzle. Put about half of the shrimp on the grill, and cook until the shrimp are curled and lightly browned, 2 to 4 minutes per side. Remove the shrimp to a plate, and repeat with the remaining shrimp.
**2.** To serve, skewer each shrimp with a cocktail toothpick. Add an onion or olive, if desired, and arrange the shrimp on a serving plate. Garnish with parsley sprigs and lemon wedges. Serve immediately at room temperature or, if made ahead, cover and refrigerate for up to 8 hours.

# Grilled Shrimp with Romesco Sauce

*Romesco is a rustic savory sauce from the Catalonian region of Spain. It goes well with any number of foods: vegetables, lamb, fish, chicken, and, as here, shrimp. When you offer a plateful of grilled shrimp with a bowl of Romesco dipping sauce, be prepared to watch it disappear fast.*

*Makes 4 servings*

---

2 dried ancho chiles, cut open and seeded

⅓ cup whole natural almonds (skins on)

2 thin slices of French bread, toasted

3 medium tomatoes, peeled and coarsely chopped

½ medium red bell pepper, coarsely chopped

2 or 3 garlic cloves, chopped

½ teaspoon plus ⅛ teaspoon salt

½ teaspoon freshly ground pepper

⅛ teaspoon cayenne

⅓ cup plus 1½ tablespoons extra-virgin olive oil

¼ cup red wine vinegar

1 pound large shrimp, shelled and deveined, with tails intact

---

**1.** Put the chiles in a small bowl, and cover with boiling water. Let soak for 20 minutes, or until softened. Drain the chiles and discard the liquid.

**2.** In a small dry skillet, toast the almonds over medium-low heat, tossing, until fragrant and lightly browned. Remove the almonds to a food processor. Break the toasted bread into pieces and add to the processor. Process the nuts and bread until finely ground. Add the drained chiles, tomatoes, bell pepper, garlic, ½ teaspoon of the salt, the pepper, and the cayenne. Process to a thick puree, scraping down the sides of the bowl as needed. With the machine on, add ⅓ cup of the olive oil through the feed tube. Then add the vinegar and blend well. Scrape the Romesco sauce into a serving bowl. Set aside at room temperature for up to 2 hours or cover and refrigerate for up to 2 days.

**3.** Put the shrimp in a bowl and toss with the remaining olive oil and salt. Heat a grill pan over medium heat until hot enough to make a few drops of water sizzle. Lay the shrimp on the hot pan and cook, turning once or twice, until they are pink and curled and the outsides are flecked with brown from the grill, 3 to 4 minutes. Mound the shrimp on a serving plate with the bowl of Romesco sauce alongside for dipping.

# California Shrimp Toasts

*Sourdough bread and jalapeño peppers contrast with curry powder, soy sauce, and sesame oil in this East-West appetizer that's a guaranteed crowd pleaser. Unlike Chinese shrimp toasts, these are not fried; the piquant salad is simply piled on top.*

*Makes about 20 toasts*

---

½ pound medium shrimp, shelled and deveined
¼ cup olive oil
2 scallions, finely chopped
½ medium red bell pepper, minced
1 fresh jalapeño pepper, seeded and minced

2 teaspoons curry powder
1 teaspoon soy sauce
¼ teaspoon Asian sesame oil
2 tablespoons mayonnaise
Salt
1 sourdough baguette loaf, sliced (about 20 slices)

---

**1.** Pat the shrimp dry with paper towels. Toss them with 2 teaspoons of the olive oil. Heat a grill pan over medium heat until hot enough to make a few drops of water sizzle. Put the shrimp on the hot pan and cook, turning, until pink and curled, 3 to 4 minutes. Remove the shrimp to a plate and let cool. Chop the shrimp.

**2.** In a medium bowl, combine the scallions, bell pepper, jalapeño, curry powder, soy sauce, sesame oil, and mayonnaise. Blend well. Add the chopped shrimp and stir to mix. Season with salt to taste. Set aside or cover and refrigerate for up to 6 hours before serving.

**3.** Shortly before serving, brush the bread slices on both sides with the remaining olive oil. Heat a grill pan over medium heat until hot enough to make a few drops of water sizzle. Put the bread on the hot pan and toast, turning, until crisp with brown grill marks, about 3 minutes. To serve, top each toast with about 1 tablespoon of the shrimp salad. Arrange on a plate and serve at once.

# Grilled Jalapeño Peppers with Tuna Stuffing

*These really do sound too simple to be true, but trust me, it's hard to make enough to keep up with the demand. The creamy tuna balances the heat of the jalapeño peppers, which retain a pleasing crunchiness after grilling. Look for the new varieties of extra-large jalapeños for this recipe.*

*Makes 4 to 6 servings*

---

12 large fresh jalapeño peppers, about 3½ inches long

1 (6-ounce) can water-packed all-white albacore tuna

2½ tablespoons mayonnaise

Salt

2 thin slices of ripe tomato, finely diced

---

**1.** With a very sharp small knife, cut the jalapeños in half lengthwise, including the stems where possible. Scoop out all the seeds and remove the white ribs. Put the jalapeño halves in a bowl of cold salted water and let stand for about 1 hour. (Soaking helps reduce the heat in the jalapeños.) If they are mild or if you like them fiery, skip this step.

**2.** Meanwhile, in a medium bowl, combine the tuna and mayonnaise. Mix to blend well. Cover and refrigerate.

**3.** Remove the jalapeños from the water and pat dry with paper towels. Heat a grill pan over medium heat until hot enough to make a few drops of water sizzle. Lay the jalapeños on the hot pan, cut sides down, and cook for 3 minutes. Turn the jalapeños over and cook the skin sides until the jalapeños are flecked with brown from the grids of the pan.

**4.** Remove the jalapeños to a flat work surface. Season the inside of each lightly with salt. Fill the cavities with the tuna. Arrange the stuffed jalapeños on a serving plate. Decorate each jalapeño half with a few bits of diced tomato.

# Rosemary Tuna Brochettes with Toasted Garlic Mayonnaise

*Using rosemary branches as aromatic skewers for grilling is a traditional Italian technique. The fragrant herb permeates the fish or meat with its heady perfume as it toasts over the coals. If you have a rosemary plant in your yard, cut branches that are sturdy enough to act as skewers but not too thick. If fresh branches are not available, use bamboo skewers and add ¾ teaspoon minced fresh rosemary to the mayonnaise.*

*Makes 4 servings*

---

6 unpeeled garlic cloves
¾ cup mayonnaise
1 tablespoon chopped parsley
1 teaspoon fresh lemon juice
Dash of cayenne
8 rosemary branches, about 5 inches long, or short bamboo skewers

1 pound fresh tuna, about 1 inch thick, cut into 16 (1-inch) pieces
2 tablespoons olive oil
½ teaspoon salt
¼ teaspoon freshly ground pepper

---

**1.** Heat a grill pan over medium heat until hot enough to make a few drops of water sizzle. Put the garlic cloves still in their skins on the hot pan. Reduce the heat to medium-low and toast the garlic, turning occasionally, until the skins are flecked with brown and the cloves feel soft when pinched with your fingers, 10 to 15 minutes. Squeeze the garlic into a blender or small food processor. Add the mayonnaise, parsley, lemon juice, and cayenne. Puree until smooth. Transfer the mayonnaise to a small bowl. Cover and refrigerate if not serving within 15 minutes.

**2.** Strip the green needles off about 3 inches of the rosemary branches, leaving about 2 inches of green attached to the tops. Put the tuna chunks in a medium bowl. Add the olive oil, salt, and pepper. Toss to coat the tuna with the oil. Thread 2 pieces of tuna onto each rosemary branch.

**3.** Heat a grill pan over medium heat until hot enough to make a few drops of water sizzle. Lay the brochettes of tuna on the pan, in batches if necessary, so they are not crowded, and grill, turning, until browned outside and cooked to medium rare inside, 4 to 6 minutes, or longer for desired degree of doneness. Transfer to a serving platter. Cook the remaining skewers in the same way. Serve hot or warm on the skewers, with the toasted garlic mayonnaise for dipping.

# Turkey Nuggets with Grilled Red Onion Dipping Sauce

*Boneless turkey breast is widely available, and I find it useful for any number of culinary purposes. These grilled turkey nuggets make a fine addition to a party buffet, or they can be passed as a hot hors d'oeuvre. Crisp tortilla chips and cold beer go well with these.*

*Makes 4 to 6 servings*

1 large red onion (about 12 ounces), sliced
3 tablespoons vegetable oil
½ cup fresh orange juice
2 tablespoons unseasoned rice vinegar
3 tablespoons red jalapeño jelly

½ teaspoon salt
¼ teaspoon freshly ground pepper
1 pound boneless turkey breast meat
1 large garlic clove, finely chopped
1 tablespoon chili powder

**1.** Brush the onion slices with 2 tablespoons of the oil. Heat a grill pan over medium heat until hot enough to make a few drops of water sizzle. Set the onion slices on the hot pan, in batches if necessary, and grill, turning, until the slices are softened and lightly browned, 3 to 5 minutes.

**2.** Put the grilled onion in a food processor or blender. Add the orange juice and vinegar and puree until smooth. Transfer to a small nonreactive saucepan. Add the jelly, salt, and pepper. Cook, stirring, until the jelly is completely melted. Reduce the heat to low and continue to cook, uncovered, stirring frequently, until the sauce thickens, 4 to 5 minutes. Remove from the heat and set aside, covered, to keep warm.

**3.** Cut the turkey into uniform bite-size pieces (about 1 inch). Put the turkey pieces in a medium bowl. Add the garlic, chili powder, and the remaining 1 tablespoon of oil. Toss to coat the turkey nuggets.

**4.** Heat a grill pan again over medium heat until hot enough to make a few drops of water sizzle. Put the turkey pieces on the pan, pushing them close together, and cook, turning once or twice, until brown on the outside and no longer pink in the center, 4 to 5 minutes. Transfer the turkey nuggets to a shallow serving dish. Pour the grilled onion sauce into a small bowl and pass on the side. Provide cocktail toothpicks for dipping the turkey into the sauce.

# Chicken Tenders with Spicy Barbecue Sauce

*The tenderloin part of the chicken breast, called tenders, can be purchased separately in most supermarket poultry sections. They make wonderful snacks. In this recipe, the tenders are presented with barbecue sauce for dipping.*

*Makes 4 servings*

---

1½ tablespoons vegetable oil

2 medium shallots, minced

1 teaspoon dried oregano

½ cup ketchup

3 tablespoons Worcestershire sauce

2 tablespoons yellow mustard

2 tablespoons honey

2 tablespoons frozen orange juice concentrate (undiluted)

1 teaspoon finely chopped parsley

¼ teaspoon crushed hot red pepper

2 pounds chicken tenders

¾ teaspoon salt

---

**1.** In a small saucepan, heat 1½ teaspoons of the oil over medium heat. Add the shallots and oregano and cook, stirring, until the shallots are softened but not browned, about 2 minutes. Add the ketchup, Worcestershire, mustard, honey, orange juice concentrate, parsley, and hot pepper. Bring to a boil over medium heat, stirring. Cook about 1 minute. Remove from the heat and cover to keep warm. The barbecue sauce can be made up to 3 days ahead and reheated just before serving, if you prefer.

**2.** Season the chicken tenders with the salt and brush with the remaining 1 tablespoon of oil. Heat a grill pan over medium heat until hot enough to make a few drops of water sizzle. Put the tenders on the hot pan and cook, turning, until light brown on both sides and white throughout but still juicy, 4 to 6 minutes.

**3.** Reheat the sauce, if necessary. Transfer to a small decorative bowl and place in the center of a serving plate. Arrange the chicken tenders around the sauce bowl. Serve hot or warm. Provide toothpicks for spearing and dipping the chicken.

# Beef Teriyaki on a Stick

*Thin strips of beef threaded onto bamboo skewers and grilled to a mahogany brown are guaranteed to attract attention at any party. Because of the marinade, they don't even need a dipping sauce.*

*Makes about 18 to 24 appetizers*

---

¼ cup dry vermouth
¼ cup soy sauce
2 tablespoons dark brown sugar
2 tablespoons vegetable oil

2 garlic cloves, crushed through a press
¼ teaspoon freshly ground pepper
1 teaspoon rice vinegar
1 (1¼- to 1½-pound) flank steak

---

**1.** In a small saucepan, combine the vermouth, soy sauce, and brown sugar. Bring to a boil and cook, stirring, until the sugar dissolves, 1 to 2 minutes. Remove from the heat. Stir in the oil, garlic, pepper, and vinegar. Transfer the marinade to a large bowl and let cool.

**2.** Trim off any excess fat and silvery membrane from the flank steak. Slice the meat crosswise on a diagonal into thin strips. In a medium bowl, toss the meat with the marinade. Marinate for at least 2 hours at room temperature or for up to 6 hours in the refrigerator, stirring occasionally.

**3.** Remove the meat from the marinade. Working over the bowl to catch the juices, thread the meat strips onto long bamboo skewers, leaving about 3 inches of the blunt ends for handles.

**4.** Heat a grill pan over medium heat until hot enough to make a few drops of water sizzle. Put the skewers of meat on the hot pan, in batches as necessary, and grill, turning 2 to 3 times, until the meat is lightly browned and cooked through, 3 to 4 minutes. Serve warm.

# Grilled Pork Tortilla Wraps with Avocado Salsa

*Boneless pork loin cut into thin slices is seasoned, grilled, and chopped for this spicy appetizer. The pork is then wrapped in soft flour tortillas along with shredded lettuce, tomatoes, and guacamole.*

*Makes 8 filled 7-inch tortillas*

1⅓ pounds lean pork, sliced ¼ inch thick

2 large garlic cloves, finely chopped

1 tablespoon soy sauce

1 tablespoon rice vinegar

2 teaspoons sugar

1 teaspoon chipotle sauce or mashed canned chipotle chile

1 teaspoon vegetable oil

1 large ripe avocado (Hass variety preferred)

⅓ cup prepared red salsa

¼ cup finely chopped white onion

1 serrano chile, finely chopped

2 tablespoons chopped cilantro

Juice of 1 fresh lime

Salt

8 (7-inch) flour tortillas

1 cup finely shredded lettuce

**1.** Pound the pork slices lightly to flatten evenly. Put the meat in a large pie plate. In a small bowl, combine the garlic, soy, vinegar, sugar, chipotle sauce, and oil. Pour over the meat, and turn the slices several times to coat with the marinade. Marinate the meat for about 30 minutes, or for up to 2 hours.

**2.** In a medium bowl, using a fork, mash the avocado. Add the salsa, onion, serrano, cilantro, and lime juice, and stir to mix. Season to taste with salt. Set the avocado salsa aside.

**3.** Spray a grill pan with nonstick cooking spray, and then heat the pan over medium heat until hot enough to make a few drops of water sizzle. Put the seasoned meat on the heated pan, and cook, turning 2 to 3 times, until nicely browned and cooked through, 3 to 4 minutes. Remove the grilled meat to a cutting board, and chop into bite-size pieces. Scrape the chopped pork into a bowl. Gently stir in the salsa.

**4.** In a dry skillet, over medium heat, soften the tortillas, 1 at a time, by turning them over 3 to 4 times, until warm and pliable. Lay 1 tortilla on a working surface. Cover with one-eighth of the chopped grilled pork and about 2 tablespoons shredded lettuce. Roll the tortilla into a cylinder. Serve warm. Repeat with the remaining tortillas.

# Polish Kielbasa Sausage Snacks

*Convenient, fully cooked, smoked sausage can be sliced, grilled, and served on a moment's notice to appease hearty appetites. Sausage is especially good with cold beer and crusty bread. Add an assortment of mustards and pickles for extra fun.*

*Makes 4 to 6 servings*

---

| | |
|---|---|
| 1 pound fully cooked Polish kielbasa sausage | 1 French baguette, thinly sliced<br>Mustard and pickles |

---

**1.** Cut the sausage on a diagonal into ½-inch-thick slices. Heat a grill pan over medium heat until hot enough to make a few drops of water sizzle.

**2.** Lay the sausage slices on the hot pan and press the pieces down with a spatula so they make contact with the grill's surface. Cook until crusty and brown, 3 to 4 minutes. Turn the sausage pieces over and cook on the second side, 3 to 4 minutes longer.

**3.** To serve, arrange the sausage on a platter with the bread. Put the mustard and pickles in small bowls. Let guests serve themselves.

# Kefta Lamb Kebabs

*Miniature log-shaped appetizers like these, made of highly seasoned ground lamb or beef, are popular street food in the Middle East. The seasoned meat is packed around skewers and grilled. Kefta are usually served in soft bread rolls or stuffed into warm pita breads. I've also included a fresh mint sauce, which is often served with the kefta.*

*Makes 12 kebabs*

---

1 pound ground lamb or beef
½ medium onion, minced
2 tablespoons finely chopped parsley
1 tablespoon finely chopped fresh mint
1 teaspoon ground cumin
½ teaspoon salt

¼ teaspoon freshly ground pepper
¼ teaspoon cinnamon
¼ teaspoon ground allspice
⅛ teaspoon grated nutmeg
Fresh Mint Sauce (recipe follows)

---

**1.** In a large bowl, combine the lamb, onion, parsley, mint, cumin, salt, pepper, cinnamon, allspice, and nutmeg. Using your hands, knead the ingredients together until very well mixed. A food processor can also be used to mix by pulsing the ingredients 10 to 12 times, but be careful not to grind the meat to a paste. Let the seasoned meat stand at room temperature for 1 hour.

**2.** With wet hands, divide the meat into 24 equal pieces and roll into sausage shapes. Pack the meat around 12 long bamboo or small metal skewers, putting 2 pieces on each skewer and leaving a 1-inch space between the pieces.

**3.** Heat a grill pan over medium heat until hot enough to make a few drops of water sizzle. Lay the skewered kefta on the heated pan and cook, turning 2 to 3 times, until brown on the outside and barely pink in the center, 6 to 8 minutes total. Serve hot, with the mint sauce on the side.

# Fresh Mint Sauce

*Makes about ½ cup*

¼ cup loosely packed coarsely chopped fresh mint

2 tablespoons coarsely chopped parsley or fresh cilantro

1 tablespoon chopped white onion

1 garlic clove, chopped

3 tablespoons fresh lemon juice

1 tablespoon unseasoned rice vinegar

⅛ teaspoon hot red chile flakes

½ teaspoon salt

In a blender or small food processor, combine all the ingredients. Puree to a sauce consistency. Pour into a small serving bowl. Use as a dipping sauce or spoon over the kefta.

## Chapter Two
# Grilled Salads

Contemporary salads are much more than a chunk of watery lettuce bathed in a boring dressing. Today's popular salads might be an artful composition of fresh ingredients beautifully arranged on an oversize plate or a shallow bowl filled with an amazing assortment of dressed baby greens. In either case, the star of the salad is likely to be grilled vegetables, meat, chicken, or seafood.

The California grilling influence has become an important part of nouvelle salads. Grilled chicken, duck, fish, shrimp, and steak are just a few of the ingredients featured in the first-course and full-meal salads in this chapter. Unusual combinations of fruits and vegetables, cooked or raw, are used in imaginative and delicious ways to create the kinds of tempting salads never dreamed of in the past. By using a stove-top grill pan, home cooks can duplicate some of these superstar salads in their own kitchens.

The recipes in this chapter use the grill pan to good advantage to create hot or cold salads that are truly different. There are complete light meal salads like Grilled Fresh Tuna Salad Niçoise or Char-Grilled Chicken with Asian Noodle Salad. Salads to serve on the side include Grilled Corn, Red Bell Pepper, and Black Bean Salad; Cauliflower Salad with Oregon Hazelnut Dressing; and Grilled Eggplant Salad with Tomato, Basil, and Feta Cheese. Just select a recipe, and put the grill pan to work.

# Asparagus Salad with Orange and Black Olive Dressing

*This unusual combination of flavors looks as stunning as it tastes. Best of all, the asparagus can be cooked ahead, so the salad is ready to go when you are ready to eat.*

*Makes 4 servings*

---

1 medium navel orange, peeled and cut into ½-inch pieces

3 tablespoons fresh orange juice

1 tablespoon finely chopped flat-leaf parsley

3 tablespoons olive oil

2 teaspoons fresh lemon juice

½ teaspoon Dijon mustard

¼ teaspoon salt

Generous grind of pepper

1 pound medium asparagus, tough ends removed

4 large romaine lettuce leaves

¼ cup canned chopped black olives

---

**1.** Put the orange pieces into a small bowl and set aside. Put the orange juice into another small bowl and add the parsley, 2 tablespoons of the olive oil, the lemon juice, mustard, half the salt, and the pepper. Whisk with a fork to blend.

**2.** In a large pot of boiling water, cook the asparagus for 1 minute only; it will finish cooking on the grill pan. Drain immediately and rinse under cold running water. Drain and blot well with paper towels to remove excess moisture. Drizzle the remaining 1 tablespoon of oil over the asparagus and roll to coat with oil. Sprinkle the asparagus with the remaining salt.

**3.** Heat a grill pan over medium heat until hot enough to make a few drops of water sizzle. Put the asparagus on the hot pan and cook until grill marks appear, 3 to

4 minutes. Turn the spears over and cook 2 minutes longer for crisp-tender spears. Transfer the asparagus to a plate to cool.

**4.** To serve, put 1 romaine leaf on each of 4 salad plates. Arrange the asparagus spears equally among the plates. Drizzle equal amounts of dressing over the salads. Sprinkle one-quarter of the chopped olives and one-quarter of the reserved orange pieces over each salad. Serve at room temperature.

# Grilled Corn, Red Bell Pepper, and Black Bean Salad

*Since there's no mayonnaise or egg in this salad and little that can spoil, it is particularly appropriate for picnics and tailgate parties.*

*Makes 4 servings*

---

2 ears of corn, shucked

2 tablespoons vegetable oil

1 large red bell pepper, quartered

1 (15-ounce) can black beans, drained and rinsed

2 scallions, chopped

1 large ripe tomato, chopped

1 fresh jalapeño pepper, seeded and minced

¼ cup slivered fresh basil

3 tablespoons extra-virgin olive oil

1 tablespoon red wine vinegar

1 tablespoon prepared thick and chunky red salsa

½ teaspoon ground cumin

½ teaspoon salt

¼ teaspoon freshly ground pepper

---

**1.** In a pot of boiling water, cook the corn for 1 minute; drain. While it is still hot, brush the corn with some of the vegetable oil. Brush the pieces of bell pepper all over with the vegetable oil.

**2.** Heat a grill pan over medium heat until hot enough to make a few drops of water sizzle. Put the corn and bell pepper on the hot pan, tent loosely with aluminum foil, and cook, turning occasionally and moving the vegetables around for even browning, until the corn is flecked with brown and the bell pepper is crisp-tender and marked from the grill, about 8 minutes.

**3.** When the corn is cool enough to handle, cut the kernels off the cobs and put into a large bowl. Cut the bell pepper into ¼-inch dice and add to the corn. Add the black beans, scallions, tomato, jalapeño, and basil. Toss to mix.

**4.** In a small bowl, whisk together the olive oil, vinegar, salsa, cumin, salt, and black pepper. Pour over the salad and stir well to combine. Season with additional salt and pepper to taste. If making ahead, cover and refrigerate for up to 6 hours for best flavor and texture. Serve at room temperature or slightly chilled.

# Cauliflower Salad with
# Oregon Hazelnut Dressing

*This salad knows no season, and neither does the stove-top grill pan. The salad ingredients are always available, and it makes a beautiful addition to a holiday meal.*

*Makes 4 servings*

---

¼ cup coarsely chopped toasted
hazelnuts
¼ cup plus 1 tablespoon olive oil
2 tablespoons raspberry or red wine
vinegar
Salt and freshly ground pepper

½ pound cauliflower florets
½ red bell pepper, cut into thin 2-inch-
long strips
½ green bell pepper, cut into thin
2-inch-long strips

---

**1.** In a medium bowl, mix the nuts, ¼ cup of the olive oil, and the vinegar. Season lightly with salt and pepper.

**2.** Cut the large pieces of cauliflower in half and leave the small florets whole. Toss the cauliflower with the remaining 1 tablespoon of olive oil.

**3.** Heat a grill pan over medium heat until hot enough to make a few drops of water sizzle. Put the cauliflower on the hot pan, pushing the pieces close together. Sprinkle with salt and pepper. Cover with a sheet of aluminum foil and cook until the pieces are flecked with brown on the bottom, 3 to 4 minutes. With tongs, turn the pieces over, reduce the heat to medium-low, cover again with foil, and cook until crisp-tender, about 2 minutes.

**4.** Remove the cauliflower to a large bowl, and, while still warm, pour on the hazelnut dressing. Add the bell peppers and toss gently to coat. Arrange the salad in a shallow bowl and serve at room temperature.

# Grilled Eggplant Salad with Tomato, Basil, and Feta Cheese

*Select a well-formed and solid globe eggplant that is shiny purple. Shun any that have brown tops or that feel soft or show signs of sitting around too long. The tender grilled eggplant rounds are topped with juicy ripe tomatoes, fresh basil, and feta cheese and served at room temperature.*

*Makes 4 servings*

---

1 large purple eggplant (about 1½ pounds), peeled and cut into 8 rounds about ½ inch thick
¼ cup extra-virgin olive oil
½ teaspoon salt

¼ teaspoon freshly ground pepper
1 large ripe tomato, finely chopped
2 tablespoons slivered fresh basil
½ cup finely diced mild feta cheese
2 teaspoons red wine vinegar

---

**1.** Brush the eggplant slices with 3 tablespoons of the olive oil. Season with the salt and pepper. Heat a grill pan over medium heat until hot enough to make a few drops of water sizzle. Put the eggplant on the hot pan and cook until grill marks appear on the bottom, 2 to 3 minutes. Rotate the eggplant slices 90 degrees and cook for 1 to 2 minutes longer to make cross-hatch grill marks. Turn the pieces over and grill on the second side until the eggplant is soft, another 2 to 3 minutes. Arrange the grilled eggplant on a serving plate, overlapping the slices and putting the attractive cross-hatched side up.
**2.** In a medium bowl, stir together the tomato, basil, feta cheese, vinegar, and remaining 1 tablespoon olive oil. Spoon the tomato mixture over the eggplant slices. Serve at room temperature.

# Fennel, Mushroom, and Red Bell Pepper Salad

*A trio of grilled vegetables served over delicate baby greens makes an easy and colorful salad for just about any occasion. The grill pan imparts a delicious smoky taste to the vegetables. To help them become tender before they burn, cover the vegetables with a loose tent of aluminum foil during the last 3 to 4 minutes of cooking.*

*Makes 4 servings*

---

1 medium fennel bulb
1 medium red bell pepper, cut lengthwise into ⅜-inch strips
8 medium mushrooms, stemmed and wiped clean
⅓ cup extra-virgin olive oil

¼ teaspoon salt
⅛ teaspoon freshly ground pepper
2 tablespoons fresh lemon juice
1½ teaspoons balsamic vinegar
6 cups baby salad greens

---

**1.** Cut off 8 sprigs of lacy fennel fronds and reserve them for garnish. Cut the stalks off the fennel bulb and discard. With a vegetable peeler, trim the tough outer fibers off the fennel bulb. Trim off a thin slice from the root end of the bulb. Slice the fennel bulb lengthwise into equal pieces about ¾ inch thick.

**2.** In a medium bowl, toss the fennel slices, bell pepper strips, and mushroom caps with 2 tablespoons of the olive oil and the salt and pepper.

**3.** Heat a grill pan over medium heat until hot enough to make a few drops of water sizzle. Put the fennel, bell pepper, and mushrooms close together on the hot pan and grill, turning 2 or 3 times, until the mushrooms are tender, about 6 minutes. Remove the mushrooms. Loosely tent the bell pepper and fennel with aluminum foil and continue cooking until they are tender, about 2 more minutes for the pepper and 4 to 5 minutes for the fennel.

---

**4.** Cut the mushrooms in half and put them in a shallow bowl along with any juices they exude. Add the grilled pepper and fennel to the mushrooms. In a small bowl, whisk together the lemon juice, balsamic vinegar, salt, pepper, and remaining olive oil. Drizzle 1 tablespoon of the dressing over the grilled vegetables and mix gently to coat.

**5.** In a large bowl, toss the salad greens with the remaining dressing. Divide the greens among 4 large plates. Top with the grilled vegetables and garnish each salad with the reserved fennel fronds.

# Grilled Leek Salad

*Here's a Mediterranean hors d'oeuvre, which translates beautifully to this country, especially in spring and summer, when thinner, more tender versions of the mild onion are available in farmers' markets. To speed grilling, the leeks are first simmered in boiling water for a few minutes.*

*Makes 4 servings*

---

4 medium leeks, no more than 1 inch across

¼ cup extra-virgin olive oil

½ teaspoon salt

2 teaspoons fresh lemon juice

3 or 4 grinds of pepper

1 hard-cooked egg, peeled and shredded (optional)

1 tablespoon chopped flat-leaf parsley

---

**1.** Cut the dark green tops off the leeks, leaving on about 2 inches of the pale green. Trim a thin slice off the root ends, keeping the bases intact. Cut the leeks in half lengthwise. Rinse them very well to remove any sand or grit hidden in the leaves. Bring a wide skillet half filled with water to a boil. Add the leeks to the boiling water, reduce the heat to low, and simmer until they are barely tender when pierced with the tip of a knife, about 5 minutes. Drain the leeks and put them on a plate. Blot with paper towels to remove excess water. Brush the leeks on both sides with 1 tablespoon of the olive oil. Season with the salt.

**2.** Heat a grill pan over medium heat until hot enough to make a few drops of water sizzle. Lay the leeks on the hot pan, cut sides down, and cook until marked with brown from the grill, 3 to 4 minutes. With tongs or a spatula, turn over and cook the second side until brown grill marks appear and the leeks are tender, 2 to 3 minutes. Transfer the leeks to a serving plate and let cool for about 5 minutes.

**3.** Drizzle the lemon juice and remaining 3 tablespoons olive oil over the warm leeks. Season with pepper and garnish with the hard-cooked egg and the parsley. Serve warm or at room temperature.

# Portobello Mushroom, Zucchini, and Onion Salad with Roquefort Dressing

*A delicious trio of pan-grilled vegetables combined with ripe tomatoes and mixed greens and topped with a creamy Roquefort dressing makes a memorable salad.*

*Makes 4 servings*

---

¼ cup plus 3 tablespoons olive oil
1 tablespoon white wine vinegar
¼ cup crumbled Roquefort cheese
¼ cup plain yogurt
3 medium portobello mushrooms, about 3 inches in diameter, stemmed and wiped clean

2 medium onions, sliced into rounds ½ inch thick
2 medium zucchini, sliced on the diagonal ¼ inch thick
Salt and freshly ground pepper
4 cups mixed salad greens
2 medium tomatoes, cut into wedges

---

**1.** In a medium bowl, mix together ¼ cup of the olive oil with the vinegar, Roquefort cheese, and yogurt. Whisk until blended.

**2.** With a melon-baller or teaspoon, scoop out the gills from the mushroom caps. Brush the mushrooms and the onions with 2 tablespoons of the olive oil. Put the zucchini slices in a bowl and toss with the remaining 1 tablespoon of oil. Season the vegetables with salt and pepper to taste.

**3.** Heat a grill pan over medium heat until hot enough to make a few drops of water sizzle. Put the mushrooms and onions on the hot pan. Cover loosely with a sheet of aluminum foil and cook, turning, until tender and brown on both sides, about 4 minutes per side. Remove the mushrooms to a cutting board and cut crosswise into ½-inch-thick slices. Separate the onions into rings.

**4.** Put the zucchini on the same grill pan and cover loosely with the foil. Cook, turning 2 to 3 times, until marked from the grill and crisp-tender, about 4 minutes total.

**5.** To assemble the salad, put the greens into a large bowl and toss with half of the Roquefort dressing. Mound the salads on 4 large plates. Arrange the grilled mushrooms, onions, and zucchini on top of the greens. Spoon an equal amount of the remaining dressing on top of each salad. Garnish each salad with tomato wedges and serve.

# Chopped Vegetable Salad with Grilled Fennel

*Grilled fennel has a tantalizing nutty flavor. Serve this intriguing salad with roasted or grilled meats. It also makes a fine vegetarian main course for two.*

*Makes 4 servings*

2 medium fennel bulbs
3 tablespoons olive oil
½ teaspoon salt
2 teaspoons white wine vinegar
1 teaspoon Dijon mustard
¼ teaspoon freshly ground pepper

2 cups coarsely chopped romaine lettuce
1 cup cooked corn kernels, fresh or frozen
½ medium red bell pepper, chopped into ½-inch pieces
1 tablespoon chopped parsley

**1.** Cut the stalks and fronds off the fennel bulbs and discard. Slice about ⅛ inch off the root ends of the fennel bulbs. Quarter the fennel bulbs lengthwise, leaving the center cores attached. Brush the fennel with 1 tablespoon of the olive oil.

**2.** Heat a grill pan over medium heat until hot enough to make a few drops of water sizzle. Put the fennel quarters on the hot pan and cook, turning 3 to 4 times, until the fennel is crisp-tender and browned with grill marks, 7 to 8 minutes total. Transfer the fennel to a plate and season with ¼ teaspoon of the salt. Let cool about 10 minutes, then chop into ½-inch pieces.

**3.** In a small bowl, whisk together the vinegar, mustard, and the remaining 2 tablespoons of olive oil. Season with the black pepper and remaining ¼ teaspoon salt. Put the romaine lettuce, corn, bell pepper, and parsley in a salad bowl. Add the chopped grilled fennel and the vinaigrette. Toss gently to combine the ingredients and coat them with the dressing.

# Pacific Rim Shrimp and Noodle Salad

*A welcome warm weather entrée salad combines grilled shrimp with cold noodles and an Asian dressing. Somen noodles are available in the Asian foods section of most supermarkets.*

*Makes 4 servings*

---

¼ cup soy sauce

2 tablespoons rice vinegar

1 tablespoon vegetable oil

1 teaspoon Asian sesame oil

1 teaspoon grated fresh ginger

1 garlic clove, finely chopped

2 teaspoons sugar

½ teaspoon salt

1 pound thin dried Japanese somen noodles

1 pound medium shrimp, shelled and deveined

2 scallions, chopped

1 carrot, peeled and shredded

3 tablespoons slivered fresh basil

---

**1.** In a small bowl, combine the soy sauce, vinegar, vegetable oil, sesame oil, ginger, garlic, sugar, and salt. Stir to dissolve the sugar.

**2.** Bring about 4 quarts of salted water to a boil in a large pot. Add the noodles. When the water returns to a boil, cook the noodles, 2½ to 3 minutes, or until tender. Drain the noodles in a colander and rinse under running water to cool; drain well. Put the drained noodles into a large bowl. Whisk the reserved dressing briefly and pour it over the noodles. Toss to coat with the dressing.

**3.** Coat a grill pan with nonstick cooking spray, then heat over medium heat until hot enough to make a few drops of water sizzle. Put the shrimp on the hot pan and cook, turning once or twice, until the shrimp are curled and pink and flecked with brown from the grill, 3 to 4 minutes.

**4.** Add the grilled shrimp and the remaining ingredients to the noodles and toss to mix. Cover and refrigerate the salad for at least 1 and for up to 6 hours. Serve chilled.

# Grilled Shrimp with Cabbage-Carrot Slaw

*Shrimp are perennially popular, and this Asian twist on traditional coleslaw makes a lovely salad for all seasons. It's refreshing and crunchy on a warm evening and equally satisfying as a light meal in blustery cold weather.*

*Makes 4 servings*

¼ cup soy sauce

2 tablespoons rice vinegar

2 teaspoons mirin (Japanese sweet rice wine)*

2 teaspoons fresh lemon juice

2 teaspoons ketchup

2 teaspoons sugar

2 tablespoons vegetable oil

½ teaspoon Asian sesame oil

¾ pound medium shrimp, peeled and deveined

1 medium head of cabbage (about 1½ pounds), finely shredded

2 medium carrots, peeled and shredded

2 large fresh jalapeño peppers, seeded and cut into thin julienne strips

½ cup loosely packed cilantro leaves

Salt and freshly ground pepper

**1.** In a small bowl, mix the soy sauce, vinegar, mirin, lemon juice, ketchup, and sugar. Stir to dissolve the sugar. Whisk in the vegetable oil and sesame oil to make the dressing. Put the shrimp into a medium bowl, and spoon 2 tablespoons of the dressing over the shrimp. Toss to coat. Let the shrimp marinate for about 15 minutes. Reserve the remaining dressing.

**2.** Heat a grill pan over medium heat until hot enough to make a few drops of water sizzle. Put the shrimp on the hot pan and cook, turning, until the shrimp are light brown on the surface and loosely curled, 3 to 4 minutes.

**3.** Put the cabbage, carrots, jalapeños, and cilantro in a large bowl. Add the reserved dressing and toss the slaw to coat. Season to taste with salt and black pepper. Mound the salad equally among 4 plates. Arrange the grilled shrimp on top. Serve warm, at room temperature, or chilled.

*Mirin can be found in the Asian food sections of many supermarkets and in Japanese food stores. It is usually located near the rice vinegar.

# Melon, Avocado, and Grilled Shrimp Salad

*This salad is a prime example of how to take advantage of the summer melon crop. Include two or more varieties of juicy sweet melons for more complex flavor and attractive color contrasts. I call for medium shrimp here because they offer more shrimp for less money. For a dramatic presentation, you can, of course, use jumbo shrimp. In that case, be sure to buy at least a dozen (even if that adds up to more than ¾ pound), to offer a minimum of three per person, and grill them an extra minute or two to allow for their greater thickness.*

*Makes 4 servings*

---

¾ pound medium shrimp, shelled and deveined

3 tablespoons plus 2 teaspoons vegetable oil

1 teaspoon soy sauce

1 garlic clove, crushed through a press

½ medium cantaloupe, rind removed, cut into ½-inch pieces

½ medium honeydew melon, rind removed, cut into ½-inch pieces

1 large avocado (preferably Hass), cut into ½-inch dice

8 to 10 large romaine lettuce leaves, torn into bite-size pieces

3 tablespoons coarsely chopped cilantro

2 tablespoons chopped fresh mint

2 tablespoons fresh lime juice

2 teaspoons rice vinegar

¼ teaspoon salt

⅛ teaspoon freshly ground pepper

---

**1.** In a medium bowl, toss the shrimp with 2 teaspoons of the oil, the soy sauce, and the garlic. Marinate for 15 to 20 minutes.

**2.** Heat a grill pan over medium heat until hot enough to make a few drops of water sizzle. Remove the shrimp from the marinade and put them on the hot pan. Cook, turning once or twice, until the outside is flecked with brown and the inside is just opaque, 3 to 4 minutes total. Remove the shrimp to a plate and let cool for 5 to 10 minutes.

**3.** Put the cantaloupe, honeydrew, avocado, lettuce, cilantro, and mint into a large bowl. In a small bowl, whisk together the remaining 3 tablespoons oil, lime juice, vinegar, salt, and pepper. Pour the vinaigrette over the salad. Toss gently to mix. Divide the salad among 4 large plates. Arrange the shrimp on top and serve.

# Salmon, Avocado, and Jicama Salad
# with Citrus Vinaigrette

*All along the Pacific coast, the popularity of salmon is reflected in imaginative dishes. This salad is an example of how versatile salmon is. It's made by grilling boneless fillets and serving them atop mixed greens with avocado, jicama, and tomato. A citrus dressing pulls all the flavors together.*

*Makes 4 servings*

---

¼ cup vegetable oil

1 tablespoon frozen orange juice concentrate, thawed

2 teaspoons fresh lime juice

¾ teaspoon salt

1 (1- to 1¼-pound) salmon fillet, about ½ inch thick, skinned and cut into 4 equal pieces

2 teaspoons olive oil

8 cups mixed salad greens

1 large avocado, peeled and cut into ¾-inch pieces

1 large ripe tomato, cut into ¾-inch pieces

½ red bell pepper, cut crosswise into ¼-inch strips

½ medium jicama, peeled and cut into thin strips ¼ inch by 2 inches

---

**1.** In a medium bowl, whisk together the vegetable oil, orange juice concentrate, lime juice, and ¼ teaspoon salt. Set the citrus dressing aside.

**2.** Heat a grill pan over medium heat until hot enough to make a few drops of water sizzle. Brush the salmon with the olive oil and season with the remaining ½ teaspoon salt. Put the salmon on the hot pan and cook until grill marks appear on the bottom, 3 to 4 minutes. Turn over and cook until the salmon is just opaque throughout, 3 to 4 minutes longer. Remove the salmon to a plate. Spoon ½ teaspoon of the citrus dressing over each piece of salmon.

**3.** In a large bowl, toss the salad greens with the avocado, tomato, bell pepper, and jicama lightly to mix. Pour on the remaining citrus dressing and toss gently to coat with the dressing. Mound one-fourth of the salad on each of 4 large plates. Put a piece of salmon on top of each salad and serve.

# Grilled Fresh Tuna Salad Niçoise

*Fresh tuna steaks turn this popular salad into a dish fit for the finest occasions. It's best in summer, when garden-ripe tomatoes and baby green beans are readily available. Serve with crusty French bread.*

*Makes 4 servings*

---

1 garlic clove, minced

3 tablespoons red wine vinegar

½ teaspoon Dijon mustard

½ cup plus 2 teaspoons extra-virgin olive oil

3 tablespoons slivered fresh basil

¾ teaspoon salt

¼ teaspoon freshly ground pepper

½ pound small fresh green beans

8 to 10 baby red new potatoes, scrubbed

2 (6- to 7-ounce) fresh tuna steaks, cut ¾ inch thick

1 red bell pepper, halved lengthwise and cut crosswise into ¼-inch-wide strips

Romaine lettuce leaves

2 medium tomatoes, cut into wedges

2 hard-cooked eggs, quartered

12 black Niçoise or kalamata olives

---

**1.** In a small bowl, mix the garlic with the vinegar and mustard. Gradually whisk in ½ cup of the olive oil until well blended. Stir in the basil and season the vinaigrette with ¼ teaspoon of the salt and ⅛ teaspoon of the pepper.

**2.** In a medium pan of boiling salted water, cook the green beans until crisp-tender, 4 to 6 minutes. With a slotted spoon, remove the beans to a colander and rinse under cold running water. Drain the beans and set aside.

**3.** In the same pot of boiling water, cook the potatoes until tender, about 10 to 15 minutes. Drain and cool the potatoes under cold running water. Cut the potatoes into halves or quarters and set aside in a separate bowl.

**4.** Season the tuna with the remaining ½ teaspoon salt and ⅛ teaspoon pepper. Coat a grill pan with nonstick cooking spray, then heat over medium heat until hot enough to make a few drops of water sizzle. Brush the tuna with the remaining 2 teaspoons of olive oil and put on the hot pan. Cook until brown grill marks appear on the bottom, 3 to 4 minutes. Turn the tuna over and cook until the fish is just opaque inside, 2 to 3 minutes. Remove the tuna to a cutting board. Let stand for 2 to 3 minutes, then cut crosswise into ½-inch-thick slices.

**5.** To assemble the salad, toss the green beans with 2 tablespoons of the vinaigrette, toss the potatoes with 2 tablespoons of vinaigrette, and toss the bell pepper with 1 tablespoon of vinaigrette. Line a large platter with lettuce leaves. Arrange the tuna slices in the center. Arrange the beans, potatoes, and pepper separately in an attractive pattern around the tuna. Moisten the tuna with about 1 tablespoon of the vinaigrette. Arrange the tomatoes, eggs, and olives at random on top of the salad. Put the remaining dressing in a small serving bowl and pass separately.

# Cajun Hot Chicken Salad

*Cold, crisp iceberg lettuce contrasts in this salad with spicy chicken and colorful bell peppers hot off the grill pan. Serve with corn bread and cold beer.*

*Makes 4 servings*

---

1 head of iceberg lettuce, torn into pieces

2 scallions (white and 2 inches of green), sliced into thin rounds

¼ cup loosely packed chopped fresh dill

2 tablespoons chopped parsley

4 skinless, boneless chicken breast halves

1½ teaspoons paprika

½ teaspoon salt

½ teaspoon freshly ground black pepper

½ teaspoon cayenne

¼ teaspoon dried thyme

¼ teaspoon powdered mustard

3 tablespoons olive oil

1 large green bell pepper, cut into strips about ½ inch wide

1 large red bell pepper, cut into strips about ½ inch wide

About ⅓ cup vinaigrette dressing (homemade or bottled)

---

**1.** In a large bowl, toss together the lettuce, scallions, dill, and parsley. Cover the bowl and refrigerate.

**2.** Cut the chicken breasts crosswise into ¾-inch-wide strips; place in a medium bowl. In a small bowl, mix the paprika, salt, black pepper, cayenne, thyme, and mustard. Sprinkle the spice mixture over the chicken and toss to coat with the spices. Add half of the olive oil and toss again. In another bowl, toss the bell pepper strips with the remaining olive oil.

**3.** Heat a grill pan over medium heat until hot enough to make a few drops of water sizzle. Lay the chicken pieces on the pan and cook, turning with tongs 3 or 4 times, until lightly colored and no longer pink inside, 4 to 5 minutes. Remove the chicken to a large bowl.

**4.** Put the bell peppers on the same hot grill pan and cook, moving and turning with tongs, until crisp-tender, 2 to 3 minutes total. Add the peppers to the bowl with the chicken pieces. Toss together.

**5.** Remove the lettuce salad from the refrigerator and toss with just enough vinaigrette to coat lightly. Divide the salad equally among 4 plates. Mound the chicken and peppers on top of each salad. Serve at once.

# Char-Grilled Chicken with Asian Noodle Salad

*Asian noodle dishes tend to be low in fat and high in taste appeal. Marinate the chicken chunks and make the noodle salad in advance. Then grill the chicken just before serving.*

*Makes 4 servings*

---

4 skinless, boneless chicken breast halves
2 tablespoons dark brown sugar
2½ tablespoons soy sauce
1½ tablespoons vegetable oil
1 tablespoon fresh lemon juice
2 garlic cloves, thinly sliced
¼ cup rice vinegar
1½ teaspoons sugar
1 teaspoon Asian toasted sesame oil
½ teaspoon salt
¼ teaspoon crushed hot red pepper

8 ounces fresh Chinese egg noodles or
    linguine
Juice of 2 limes
¼ cup chopped fresh cilantro
¼ cup chopped fresh mint
2 medium tomatoes, chopped
2 scallions, finely chopped
1 medium carrot, shredded
½ medium cucumber, peeled, quartered
    lengthwise, seeded, and thinly sliced
    crosswise

---

**1.** Cut the chicken breasts crosswise into 1-inch strips. In a medium bowl, mix the brown sugar, 2 tablespoons of the soy sauce, 1 tablespoon of the vegetable oil, the lemon juice, and the garlic. Add the chicken, stir to coat with the marinade, cover, and refrigerate, stirring once or twice, for 2 to 4 hours.

**2.** To make the noodle dressing, in a small bowl, combine the vinegar, sugar, sesame oil, salt, hot pepper, and the remaining 1½ teaspoons each of vegetable oil and soy sauce. Whisk to blend well.

**3.** In a large pot, bring 4 quarts of salted water to a boil. With your hands, separate the noodle strands and add them to the boiling water. Stir while the water returns to a boil. Cook 3 to 5 minutes, testing often, until the noodles are just tender to the bite. Immediately empty the noodles into a colander and rinse under cold water. Drain the noodles well and put them in a large bowl. Add the dressing, lime juice, cilantro, mint, tomatoes, scallions, carrot, and cucumber. Toss gently. Cover and refrigerate for up to 4 hours.

**4.** Remove the marinated chicken from the refrigerator about 30 minutes before cooking. Heat a grill pan over medium heat until hot enough to make a few drops of water sizzle. With tongs, lift the chicken pieces from the marinade and put the pieces, nearly touching, onto the hot pan. Cook, turning several times and brushing with some of the marinade, for 4 minutes. Continue cooking and turning until the chicken is very brown on all sides, 2 to 3 minutes longer. If some of the chicken pieces begin to char before they are done, move them to a cooler part of the pan. Remove the cooked chicken to a plate.

**5.** Taste the cold noodles and season with additional salt to taste. Divide among 4 plates. Arrange the hot chicken pieces on top. Drizzle any juices that have collected on the plate over the salads and serve.

# Chicken, Kidney Bean, and Cabbage Salad with Gorgonzola Cheese

*High in fiber and low in fat, this is a nutritious main-course salad to toss together at a moment's notice.*

*Makes 4 servings*

---

1 (15-ounce) can dark red kidney beans, drained and rinsed
2 cups shredded cabbage
2 celery ribs, sliced crosswise
1 medium tomato, chopped
½ green bell pepper, cut into thin strips
2 scallions, chopped
2 tablespoons chopped parsley

1 tablespoon Dijon mustard
2 tablespoons red wine vinegar
½ teaspoon salt
¼ teaspoon freshly ground pepper
3½ tablespoons olive oil
3 skinless, boneless chicken breast halves
½ cup crumbled Gorgonzola or other blue cheese

---

**1.** In a large bowl, combine the kidney beans, cabbage, celery, tomato, bell pepper, scallions, and parsley. In a small bowl, whisk together the mustard, vinegar, and half the salt and pepper. Slowly whisk in 3 tablespoons of the olive oil until blended. Add the dressing to the salad and toss to coat.

**2.** Heat a grill pan over medium heat until hot enough to make a few drops of water sizzle. Brush the chicken breasts with the remaining ½ tablespoon oil and season with the remaining ¼ teaspoon salt and ⅛ teaspoon pepper. Lay the chicken on the hot pan and cook until brown grill marks appear on the bottom, 4 to 5 minutes. Turn the breasts over and cook the second side until white but still juicy in the center, 3 to 4 minutes longer. Remove the chicken to a cutting board and let stand for 2 to 3 minutes, then slice crosswise into strips.

**3.** To serve, mound the bean and cabbage salad equally among 4 plates. Arrange the chicken strips on top. Scatter the Gorgonzola cheese over all.

# Chicken and Spinach Salad with Apples and Chutney Dressing

*Sort of a cross between chicken curry and Waldorf salad, this dish features strips of grilled chicken arranged over a salad of baby spinach, walnuts, and crisp apple bits tossed with a chutney dressing. It is just right for a special luncheon. Serve with brioche or semolina bread and, if you like, a dry white wine.*

*Makes 6 to 8 first-course servings or 4 main-course servings*

---

¼ cup plus 2 teaspoons vegetable oil
3 tablespoons mango or peach chutney
2 tablespoons rice vinegar
1 teaspoon curry powder
1 teaspoon fresh lemon juice
½ teaspoon salt
4 skinless, boneless chicken breast halves
1 (10-ounce) package prewashed baby spinach leaves

1 head of Belgian endive, cut crosswise into ½-inch pieces
1 large firm red apple, cored and cut into ½-inch dice
1 celery rib, thinly sliced
¾ cup walnut pieces

---

**1.** In a mini food processor or blender, put ¼ cup of the oil, the chutney, vinegar, curry powder, lemon juice, and ¼ teaspoon of the salt. Puree until smooth. Transfer the dressing to a small bowl.

**2.** Put the chicken breasts between 2 sheets of plastic wrap and pound gently to an even ½-inch thickness. Brush the chicken lightly with the remaining 2 teaspoons vegetable oil and season with the remaining ¼ teaspoon salt.

**3.** Heat a grill pan over medium heat until hot enough to make a few drops of water sizzle. Lay the chicken breasts on the hot pan and cook until brown grill marks appear

---

on the bottom, 4 to 5 minutes. Turn over and cook until the chicken is white but still juicy in the center, 3 to 4 minutes longer. Transfer the chicken to a cutting board, and let stand for a few minutes.

**4.** While the chicken rests, put the spinach, endive, apple, celery, and walnuts in a large bowl. Pour the dressing over the salad and toss to coat evenly. Pile the salad on 4 large plates. Cut the chicken breasts crosswise into 1-inch strips, arrange over the salads, and serve.

# Grilled Chicken Caesar Salad

*You don't have to pay restaurant prices to enjoy this popular contemporary classic. With the stove-top grill pan, it's easy to make at home. When entertaining, grill the chicken ahead of time. Note: There is no egg in this version.*

*Makes 4 servings*

---

6 anchovy fillets, chopped
2 large garlic cloves, minced
2 teaspoons red wine vinegar
2 teaspoons Dijon mustard
½ teaspoon Worcestershire sauce
½ cup plus 1 tablespoon extra-virgin olive oil

1 large head of romaine lettuce, torn into pieces
4 skinless, boneless chicken breast halves
¼ teaspoon salt
⅛ teaspoon freshly ground pepper
1 cup croutons
½ cup freshly grated Parmesan cheese

---

**1.** In a blender, mix the anchovies, garlic, vinegar, mustard, and Worcestershire until well combined. Add ½ cup olive oil and blend until smooth. Set aside. Put the romaine lettuce into a large bowl and refrigerate.

**2.** Heat a grill pan over medium heat until hot enough to make a few drops of water sizzle. Brush the chicken breasts with the remaining 1 tablespoon oil, and sprinkle with the salt and pepper. Put the chicken on the heated pan, and cook, turning 3 or 4 times, until brown on the outside and no longer pink on the inside, 8 to 10 minutes total. Remove the chicken to a cutting board. Let stand 5 minutes, and then cut the chicken into bite-sized pieces.

**3.** Add the dressing to the lettuce and toss. Add the croutons, cheese, and chicken pieces. Toss again to mix the ingredients. Taste and season with salt and pepper. Divide the salad among 4 serving plates, and serve at once.

# Sizzling Ham, Avocado, and Tomato Salad

*Fully cooked ham browns quickly on the grill pan, so have the rest of the salad
ready and waiting before you begin.*

*Makes 4 servings*

---

1 head of romaine or green leaf lettuce,
   torn into pieces
2 medium ripe tomatoes, cut into bite-
   sized pieces
1 large avocado, quartered lengthwise,
   then cut crosswise into ¼-inch-thick
   pieces
½ medium red onion, very thinly sliced

3 tablespoons extra-virgin olive oil
1 tablespoon red wine vinegar
½ teaspoon Dijon mustard
¼ teaspoon salt
⅛ teaspoon freshly ground pepper
1 fully cooked bone-in ham steak (about
   1 pound), trimmed of all fat

---

**1.** In a salad bowl, toss the lettuce, tomatoes, avocado, and red onion. In a small bowl, whisk together the olive oil, vinegar, mustard, salt, and pepper. Set the dressing aside.
**2.** Heat a grill pan over medium heat until hot enough to make a few drops of water sizzle. Lay the ham on the hot pan and cook until brown grill marks appear on the bottom, 3 to 4 minutes. Turn the ham over and cook 2 to 3 minutes, or until hot and lightly browned. Remove the ham to a cutting board and while still hot, remove the bone and cut the ham into strips about 2 inches by ¼ inch.
**3.** Add the ham strips to the bowl with the salad. Pour the dressing over the salad and toss gently to combine.

# Beef Patty Taco Salad

*This twist on the ordinary taco salad grills tiny beef patties in place of frying crumbled ground beef. The result adds a hint of smoke and allows for extra seasoning of the meat.*

*Makes 4 servings*

---

1 pound lean ground beef

2 tablespoons minced onion

1 teaspoon Worcestershire sauce

2 teaspoons chili powder

½ teaspoon dried oregano

½ teaspoon salt

1 small head of iceberg lettuce, torn into bite-sized pieces

1 (15-ounce) can pinto beans, rinsed and drained

1 large tomato, chopped

1 large avocado, peeled and diced

1 cup crushed corn tortilla chips

¼ cup chopped cilantro

2 scallions, chopped

2 tablespoons olive oil or vegetable oil

2 teaspoons red wine vinegar

Juice of 1 lime

¼ cup plus 2 tablespoons thick and chunky red salsa

1 cup shredded cheddar cheese

¼ cup sour cream

---

**1.** In a medium bowl, combine the ground beef, onion, Worcestershire, chili powder, oregano, and salt, and mix well. Form into 16 small patties about ½ inch thick.

**2.** Heat a grill pan over medium heat until hot enough to make a few drops of water sizzle. Put the patties on the hot pan and cook until brown grill marks appear on the bottom, 3 to 4 minutes. Turn over and cook until the meat is no longer pink in the center but still juicy, 2 to 3 minutes, or to the desired degree of doneness. Leave the patties on the pan off the heat.

**3.** In a large bowl, combine the lettuce, beans, tomato, avocado, tortilla chips, cilantro, and scallions, and toss gently. Add the oil, vinegar, lime juice, and ¼ cup of the salsa. Toss again to mix.

**4.** To serve, divide the salad among 4 large plates. Arrange 4 patties on each salad and top each with one-fourth of the cheese. Garnish each salad with a drizzle of sour cream and ½ tablespoon of salsa.

# Mexican Grilled Beef Salad

*Here's a centerpiece salad that's worthy of a Mexican fiesta. The stove-top grill pan adds a wonderful smoky flavor to the beef. Serve with fresh salsa, guacamole, and soft warm tortillas to turn this into a whole meal.*

*Makes 6 servings*

1½ pounds medium red potatoes

2 large fresh poblano peppers—roasted, peeled, and cut into thin strips (see Note)

2 tablespoons finely chopped white onion

2 tablespoons rice vinegar

Juice of 1 lime

¼ cup olive oil

1 teaspoon salt

½ teaspoon freshly ground pepper

1 flank steak (about 1½ pounds), trimmed of silvery membrane and any excess fat

1 tablespoon vegetable oil

1 garlic clove, minced

½ teaspoon dried oregano, preferably Mexican

2 cups shredded romaine lettuce

½ cup crumbled queso fresco or mild feta cheese

Chopped fresh cilantro or parsley

**1.** In a medium saucepan of boiling salted water, cook the potatoes until tender, 15 to 20 minutes. Drain and rinse the potatoes under cold running water until cool enough to handle. Peel the potatoes and cut into neat ½-inch dice. Place the potatoes in a large bowl.

**2.** Add the poblano strips, onion, vinegar, lime juice, and olive oil to the potatoes. Toss to mix. Season with half the salt and black pepper.

**3.** With a sharp knife, score the steak in a diamond pattern, cutting only ⅛ to ¼ inch into the meat. Put the steak on a platter and rub all over with the vegetable oil, garlic, and oregano. Season with the remaining ½ teaspoon salt and ¼ teaspoon pepper. Let the steak stand at room temperature for about 30 minutes.

**4.** Heat a grill pan over medium heat until hot enough to make a few drops of water sizzle. Put the steak on the hot pan and cook until brown grill marks appear on the bottom, 4 to 5 minutes. Turn over and cook 3 to 4 minutes for rare, about 5 minutes for medium-rare, or longer for the desired degree of doneness. Transfer the steak to a cutting board and let stand for about 5 minutes. Cut the steak crosswise on a diagonal into ¼-inch-thick strips. Cut the strips crosswise into bite-sized pieces.

**5.** Add the grilled steak to the potatoes and poblanos. Stir gently to mix. Arrange the lettuce on a large platter. Mound the beef salad on the lettuce. Sprinkle the cheese and cilantro on top. Serve the salad at room temperature.

NOTE: Roast the poblano peppers on the grill pan, under a broiler, or directly over a gas flame until charred. Seal in a brown paper or plastic bag to steam for about 10 minutes. Then rub off the blackened skin and remove the stems and seeds and cut into strips.

# Canadian Bacon and Potato Salad

*Plan to include this hearty potato salad in your next picnic or patio supper.*

*Makes 4 servings*

---

1½ pounds medium red potatoes, peeled, quartered lengthwise, and sliced ¼ inch thick

3 tablespoons mayonnaise

2 tablespoons coarse-grained mustard

2 teaspoons white wine vinegar

2 tablespoons finely chopped onion

3 small sweet gherkin pickles, chopped

½ teaspoon salt

⅛ teaspoon freshly ground pepper

6 slices (about 4 ounces) Canadian bacon

---

**1.** In a large pot of boiling water, cook the potatoes, uncovered, until just tender, 6 to 8 minutes. Drain the potatoes and put into a large bowl. While the potatoes are still hot, add the mayonnaise, mustard, vinegar, onion, pickles, salt, and pepper. Stir gently to mix and to coat the potatoes with the dressing.

**2.** Heat a grill pan over medium heat until hot enough to make a few drops of water sizzle. Put the Canadian bacon on the hot pan and cook until brown grill marks appear on the bottom, 2 to 3 minutes. Turn the bacon over and cook the second side for 2 minutes.

**3.** Remove the bacon to a cutting board and cut into ½-inch pieces. Add to the salad and toss to combine. Serve warm or at room temperature.

# Pan-Grilled Cauliflower Salad with Red Onion Vinaigrette

*Makes 4 to 6 servings*

¼ cup olive oil
1 medium red onion, quartered and thinly sliced
1 tablespoon red wine vinegar
½ teaspoon sugar

½ teaspoon salt
¼ teaspoon freshly ground pepper
1 medium head of cauliflower, trimmed and separated into florets

**1.** In a large nonstick skillet, heat 2 tablespoons of the olive oil over medium heat. Add the red onion and cook, stirring frequently, until softened, 2 to 3 minutes. Add the vinegar and sugar. Season with the salt and pepper. Remove from the heat and set aside.

**2.** Cut the large pieces of cauliflower in half and leave the small florets whole. Toss the cauliflower with the remaining 2 tablespoons oil to coat lightly.

**3.** Heat a grill pan over medium heat until hot enough to make a few drops of water sizzle. Put the cauliflower on the heated pan, pushing the pieces close together. Sprinkle lightly with additional salt and pepper. Cover loosely with a sheet of aluminum foil and cook until the cauliflower pieces are flecked with brown on the bottom, 4 to 5 minutes. Using tongs, turn the pieces over, reduce the heat to medium-low, cover again with the foil, and cook for 3 minutes.

**4.** Arrange the cauliflower on a serving platter and spoon the onion vinaigrette on top. Let the salad cool to room temperature before serving.

*Chapter Three*

# Grilled Seafood

It may be true, as some seafood fanciers say, that many fish varieties taste better grilled than cooked any other way. Simply grilling fish and serving it with a light vinaigrette or uncomplicated sauce highlights its flavor. With a handy grill pan, the freshest catch-of-the-day is easy, healthy, and quick to prepare whenever you want.

Seafood is more popular than in the past, perhaps because much better fish is now available, thanks to fast air delivery to cities throughout the country. The recipes in this chapter show how useful the grill pan is for cooking fish simply and quickly; they also demonstrate the contemporary way of matching fish with interesting and flavorful sauces to produce such dishes as Spicy Peanut Shrimp, Bahama Mama Snapper Fillets with Plantains, Mahimahi with Pineapple Salsa, and Seared Scallops with Sweet Red Pepper Sauce and Corn.

# Grilled Catfish with Zesty Tartar Sauce

*The recent popularity of catfish might be attributed to farm-raised catfish, which are milder and sweeter than the wild kind. Catfish in the Southern style are usually served with a spicy sauce. A spicy tartar sauce is the choice here, and the fish is cooked on the stove-top grill pan rather than fried.*

*Makes 4 servings*

½ cup mayonnaise
1 tablespoon Creole or other coarse-grained mustard
1 tablespoon finely chopped parsley
1 scallion, finely chopped
2 teaspoons sweet pickle relish

2 teaspoons drained capers
¼ teaspoon Worcestershire sauce
¼ teaspoon Tabasco sauce
Salt and freshly ground pepper
4 (6-ounce) catfish fillets
2 teaspoons olive oil

**1.** In a medium bowl, combine the mayonnaise, mustard, parsley, scallion, pickle relish, capers, Worcestershire, and Tabasco. Mix very well. Season with salt and pepper to taste. Transfer the sauce to a serving bowl.

**2.** Brush the catfish with the oil and season lightly with salt and pepper. Coat a grill pan with nonstick cooking spray, then heat the pan over medium heat until hot enough to make a few drops of water sizzle. Put the catfish on the hot pan and cook until brown grill marks appear on the bottom, 3 to 4 minutes. With a wide spatula, carefully turn the fish over and cook until white inside, about 2 minutes. Serve the fish with about 1 tablespoon of the sauce spooned on top. Pass the remaining sauce on the side.

# Grilled Halibut with Ginger Butter

*Here's proof that a little butter can go a long way. Just melt a small pat enlivened with lemon zest and fresh ginger over a stove-top grilled halibut steak to enrich the flavor. This is an interpretation of a recipe by Janie Hibler, a food writer from Portland, Oregon.*

*Makes 4 servings*

---

4 tablespoons unsalted butter, softened
1 tablespoon grated fresh ginger
1 teaspoon grated lemon zest
4 (7- to 8-ounce) halibut steaks, about
   ¾ inch thick

2 teaspoons vegetable oil
½ teaspoon salt
¼ teaspoon freshly ground pepper
1 tablespoon finely chopped parsley

---

**1.** In a small bowl, work together the butter, ginger, and lemon zest with the back of a spoon until well blended. Wrap the ginger butter in plastic wrap and form into a 4-inch log. Refrigerate until firm, 1 to 2 hours.

**2.** Heat a grill pan over medium heat until hot enough to make a few drops of water sizzle. Brush the halibut lightly with the oil and season with the salt and pepper. Put the fish on the hot pan and cook until brown grill marks appear in the bottom, 4 to 5 minutes. Turn and grill the second side until brown outside and opaque in the center.

**3.** Cut the cold ginger butter into 4 equal rounds. Top each halibut steak with a round of butter. Garnish with the parsley and serve at once.

# Halibut with Jalapeno-Lime Vinaigrette

*Room-temperature vinaigrettes served as sauces over hot, freshly grilled fish have been fashionable for years. They offer a way of delivering intense flavor in a light form. Steamed basmati rice and buttered carrots and snow peas would make perfect partners for the fish.*

*Makes 4 servings*

---

½ cup lightly packed cilantro leaves
2 scallions, chopped
2 large jalapeño peppers, seeded and
   chopped
1 tablespoon finely chopped fresh ginger
1 garlic clove, chopped

3 tablespoons fresh lime juice
2 tablespoons soy sauce
2½ tablespoons vegetable oil
4 (7- to 8-ounce) halibut steaks, about
   ¾ inch thick
½ teaspoon salt

---

**1.** In a blender or small food processor, put the cilantro, scallions, jalapeños, ginger, garlic, lime juice, soy sauce, 2 tablespoons of the oil, and 3 tablespoons of water. Blend very well. Transfer to a small bowl and reserve at room temperature. For best flavor, make the vinaigrette no more than 3 hours in advance.

**2.** Brush a grill pan lightly with oil. Heat over medium heat until hot enough to make a few drops of water sizzle. Brush the halibut on both sides with the remaining ½ tablespoon of oil. Season with the salt. Put the halibut on the pan and cook until marked on the bottom with stripes from the grill, 4 to 5 minutes. Turn and cook the second side until brown on the outside and opaque in the center, 3 to 4 minutes.

**3.** Whisk the vinaigrette to blend. Pour over the warm fish and serve at once.

# Halibut with Oregano and Garlic

*This is a tasty way to cook up a delicate fish. Serve with rice or buttered new potatoes and sautéed zucchini. The sauce is drizzled over the fish just before serving.*

*Makes 4 servings*

---

1 tablespoon dried oregano
1 teaspoon finely chopped garlic
½ teaspoon salt
3½ tablespoons extra-virgin olive oil
1 tablespoon fresh lemon juice

1 tablespoon finely chopped parsley
¼ teaspoon freshly ground pepper
4 (6- to 8-ounce) halibut steaks, about
  ½ inch thick

---

**1.** With a mortar and pestle, or on a cutting board with a large knife, mash the oregano, garlic, and salt together to make a paste. Scrape the paste into a small bowl. Add 3 tablespoons of the olive oil, the lemon juice, parsley, and pepper. Whisk to blend. Set the garlic sauce aside.

**2.** Heat a grill pan over medium heat until hot enough to make a few drops of water sizzle. Brush the halibut with the remaining ½ tablespoon of olive oil and put the steaks on the hot grill pan. Cook until brown grill marks appear, 3 to 4 minutes. Turn the fish over and grill until brown on the second side and opaque in the center, 3 to 4 minutes longer. Spoon the garlic sauce over the fish and serve.

# Mahimahi with Pineapple Salsa

*Thanks to high-speed delivery to the mainland, Hawaiian mahimahi is now widely available. Its firm, white flesh grills easily, and the fish teams up deliciously with a tropical salsa. Rice makes a good accompaniment here.*

*Makes 4 servings*

½ ripe pineapple, cut into ½-inch dice
½ medium red bell pepper, cut into ¼-inch dice
1 or 2 serrano peppers, seeded and minced
2 tablespoons finely chopped white onion
1 tablespoon rice vinegar

½ teaspoon sugar
2 tablespoons chopped fresh mint
4 (6-ounce) pieces of mahimahi, about ¾ inch thick
1 tablespoon olive oil
¼ teaspoon salt
⅛ teaspoon freshly ground pepper

**1.** In a medium bowl, combine the pineapple, bell pepper, serrano, onion, vinegar, sugar, and mint. Set the pineapple salsa aside.

**2.** Brush the fish on both sides with the oil. Season with the salt and pepper. Heat a grill pan over medium heat until hot enough to make a few drops of water sizzle. Put the fish on the hot pan and cook until brown grill marks appear on the bottom, 3 to 4 minutes. Turn the fish over and grill until cooked through, about 4 minutes longer. Serve the fish with the pineapple salsa.

# Grilled Salmon with Orange Vinaigrette

*Popular and quick cooking, salmon can be prepared on the busiest of days. When you want to dress up a plain fillet, I recommend this easy orange vinaigrette. Since fish has a tendency to stick to pan surfaces, coat the grill pan with nonstick cooking spray before heating.*

*Makes 4 servings*

---

¼ cup fresh orange juice

¼ cup balsamic vinegar

2 tablespoons extra-virgin olive oil

1 anchovy fillet, minced

1 tablespoon minced shallot

1½ teaspoons grated orange zest

1½ teaspoons chopped parsley

¼ teaspoon salt

⅛ teaspoon freshly ground pepper

2 (12-ounce) salmon fillets

---

**1.** In a small bowl, combine the orange juice, vinegar, olive oil, anchovy, shallot, orange zest, parsley, salt, and pepper.

**2.** Coat a grill pan with nonstick cooking spray, then heat over medium heat until hot enough to make a few drops of water sizzle. Put the salmon fillets on the hot pan, skin side up, and cook until brown grill marks appear on the bottom, 3 to 4 minutes. Turn the fish and cook the second side until the salmon is opaque in the center, about 7 minutes. (Total cooking time will vary, depending upon the thickness of the fish.)

**3.** To serve, lift the salmon fillets right off the skin onto a platter. Cut the fillets in half, transfer to 4 serving plates, and spoon the vinaigrette over the fish. Serve warm or at room temperature.

# Salmon with Swedish Chive Cream

*A cold, creamy sauce flavored with mustard and chives tastes especially good with pink salmon fillets. For a bright, light, spring plate, serve the fish with fresh peas or asparagus and baby new potatoes.*

*Makes 4 servings*

---

1 hard-cooked egg yolk
¼ cup sour cream or plain yogurt
2 tablespoons mayonnaise
1½ tablespoons Dijon mustard

2 tablespoons finely chopped chives
Salt and freshly ground pepper
4 (6- to 7-ounce) skinless, boneless
    salmon fillets, about 1 inch thick

---

**1.** In a blender or small food processor, combine the egg yolk, sour cream, mayonnaise, mustard, and chives. Puree until smooth. Season to taste with salt and pepper. Transfer the sauce to a small bowl. If not serving shortly, cover and refrigerate.

**2.** Coat a grill pan with nonstick cooking spray, then heat over medium heat until hot enough to make a few drops of water sizzle. Season the salmon lightly with salt and pepper. Put the salmon fillets on the hot pan and cook until brown grill marks appear on the bottom, 4 to 5 minutes. Turn the fish over and cook the second side until the salmon is opaque in the center, about 5 minutes. Serve the grilled salmon with the sauce spooned on top.

# Sea Bass with Warm Mango Salsa

*Mild sea bass fillets team up with an unusual sweet-hot mango sauce that's barely cooked. It's a lovely way to enjoy the tropical flavor of fresh mango.*

*Makes 4 servings*

---

2 tablespoons butter

2 scallions, thinly sliced

1 large ripe mango, peeled and diced

¼ cup fresh lime juice

½ teaspoon sugar, or more if the mango is tart

1 serrano pepper, minced, with seeds

4 (6- to 7-ounce) sea bass fillets

2 teaspoons vegetable oil

½ teaspoon salt

1 tablespoon chopped cilantro or parsley

---

**1.** In a small skillet, melt the butter over medium heat. Add the scallions and cook, stirring, for 1 minute. Add the mango, lime juice, sugar, and serrano. Cook, tossing gently, until just heated through, 1 to 2 minutes. Set the mango salsa aside in the pan off the heat.

**2.** Coat a grill pan with nonstick cooking spray. Then heat the pan over medium heat until hot enough to make a few drops of water sizzle. Brush the fish fillets lightly with the oil and season with the salt. Put the fish on the hot pan and cook until brown grill marks appear on the bottom, 3 to 4 minutes. Turn the fish over and cook until just opaque inside, 2 to 3 minutes. Serve the fish with the warm mango salsa spooned on top. Garnish with a sprinkle of cilantro.

# Snapper Fillets with Lime Parsley Butter

*Small, thin fish fillets are particularly easy to prepare on stove-top grill pans. They cook quickly and look very appetizing with brown grill marks on the delicate white flesh. The only trick is to make sure the fillets hold together and to cook them just through. Since thin fish fillets tend to stick to the pan, it's important that the fish be very fresh and to oil both the pan and the fish before grilling.*

*Makes 2 servings*

---

2 tablespoons butter
1 small garlic clove, crushed through a
   press
1 teaspoon finely chopped parsley

2 teaspoons fresh lime juice
4 small skinned snapper fillets
1½ tablespoons vegetable oil
Salt and freshly ground pepper

---

**1.** In a small saucepan, melt the butter over medium heat. Add the garlic and cook, stirring, until softened and fragrant but not browned, 1 to 2 minutes. Stir in the parsley and lime juice. Set aside.

**2.** Brush both a grill pan and the fish fillets on both sides with the vegetable oil. Season the fish lightly with salt and pepper. Heat the grill pan over medium heat until hot enough to make a few drops of water sizzle. Lay the fish fillets on the hot pan, crosswise to the grids. Cook the fish until brown grill marks are evident on the bottom, 3 to 4 minutes. With a wide spatula, gently turn the fish over and cook the second side until the fish is opaque in the center, 1 to 2 minutes. Briefly reheat the sauce and serve spooned over the fish.

# Bahama Mama Snapper Fillets with Plantains

*Caribbean cooking has its spicy moments, and here the habanero or Scotch bonnet chile gives the marinade its required kick.*

*Makes 4 servings*

---

3 tablespoons olive oil
1 large garlic clove, chopped
2 tablespoons fresh lime juice
1 tablespoon finely chopped fresh ginger
1 habanero or Scotch bonnet chile, quartered and seeded
¼ teaspoon salt

⅛ teaspoon freshly ground pepper
4 (6- to 7-ounce) snapper fillets
1 tablespoon unsalted butter
2 medium plantains, halved crosswise, quartered lengthwise
Lime wedges

---

**1.** In a large shallow glass baking dish, mix together the olive oil, garlic, lime juice, ginger, habanero, salt, and pepper. Put the fish fillets in the dish, and turn to coat with the marinade. Let stand for 30 minutes.

**2.** Meanwhile, in a medium skillet, melt the butter over medium heat. Add the plantain quarters and cook, turning, until golden brown and tender on all sides, 6 to 8 minutes total. Season the plantains lightly with salt.

**3.** Coat a grill pan with nonstick cooking spray, then heat over medium heat until hot enough to make a few drops of water sizzle. Lift the fish from the marinade and pat dry with paper towels. Put the fish fillets on the hot pan and cook, turning once, until both sides are browned with grill marks and the fish is just opaque throughout, 2 to 3 minutes per side. Serve the fish with the plantains and lime wedges.

---

# Snapper Fillets with Saffron

*Saffron lends a subtle flavor and a yellow hue to the sauce for the snapper. This is a light and pretty dish to serve in the spring with fresh asparagus.*

*Makes 4 servings*

---

3 tablespoons olive oil

1 red bell pepper, cut into ½-inch pieces

½ medium onion, thinly sliced

4 garlic cloves, finely chopped

½ teaspoon dried oregano

¼ teaspoon crumbled saffron threads

¼ cup chicken broth

2 tablespoons dry vermouth or white wine

4 (6-ounce) red snapper or rock fish fillets, about ½ inch thick

Salt and freshly ground pepper

---

**1.** In a large skillet, heat 2 tablespoons of the oil over medium heat. Add the bell pepper, onion, and garlic. Cook, stirring, until the onion is tender, 3 to 5 minutes. Add the oregano, saffron, broth, and vermouth. Bring to a boil and cook until the liquid is reduced by half, 2 to 3 minutes. Remove from the heat and set the sauce aside.

**2.** Brush the fish with the remaining 1 tablespoon of oil. Season lightly with salt and pepper. Coat a grill pan with nonstick cooking spray, then heat over medium heat until hot enough to make a few drops of water sizzle. Put the fish on the hot pan and cook until brown grill marks appear on the bottom, 3 to 4 minutes. Gently turn the fish over and cook until the fish is opaque in the thickest part, 3 to 4 minutes longer.

**3.** Meanwhile, reheat the sauce in the skillet. Transfer the grilled snapper to plates, spoon the sauce on top, and serve.

# Fillet of Sole with Lemon Butter and Capers

*Delicate sole cooks fast and may stick to the pan, so it's very important to coat the grill pan with nonstick cooking spray and also to brush the fish fillets liberally with melted butter or oil before cooking.*

*Makes 4 servings*

---

3 tablespoons unsalted butter

1 tablespoon fresh lemon juice

1 teaspoon drained capers

4 (5- to 6-ounce) sole fillets

¼ teaspoon salt

⅛ teaspoon freshly ground pepper

---

**1.** In a small saucepan, melt 2 tablespoons of the butter over low heat. Add the lemon juice and capers. Remove from the heat and set aside, covered, to keep warm.

**2.** In a small bowl, melt the remaining 1 tablespoon of butter in a microwave oven. Brush both sides of the sole fillets with the melted butter. Season with the salt and pepper. Coat a grill pan with nonstick cooking spray, then heat the pan over medium heat until hot enough to make a few drops of water sizzle. Put the fish on the hot pan and cook until brown grill marks appear on the bottom, about 2 minutes. Gently turn the fish over and cook until opaque in the center, 1 to 2 minutes longer. Transfer to plates and drizzle the warm lemon butter over the fish, distributing the capers evenly.

# Swordfish with Tomato, Olive, and Caper Relish

*Swordfish is a luxury and worth special treatment such as this. Steamed and buttered new potatoes or rice and broccoli are good choices to serve with the fish.*

*Makes 4 servings*

---

4 (6- to 7-ounce) swordfish steaks, about ½ inch thick, with skin trimmed off
¼ cup olive oil
3 garlic cloves, finely chopped
2 teaspoons red wine vinegar

8 large pitted kalamata olives, coarsely chopped
2 medium tomatoes, chopped
2 tablespoons slivered fresh basil
1 tablespoon drained capers
Salt and freshly ground pepper

---

**1.** Put the fish in a large glass baking dish. Add 2 tablespoons of the olive oil and the garlic. Turn the fish to coat. Cover and refrigerate for 1 to 2 hours.

**2.** In a medium bowl, combine the remaining 2 tablespoons of olive oil with the vinegar. Add the olives, tomatoes, basil, and capers. Stir together. Season to taste with salt and pepper. Set aside at room temperature.

**3.** Remove the fish from the marinade and scrape off any garlic that clings to it. Season the steaks lightly with salt and pepper. Coat a grill pan with nonstick cooking spray. Heat the pan over medium heat until hot enough to make a few drops of water sizzle. Put the fish on the hot pan and cook until brown grill marks appear on the bottom, 3 to 4 minutes. Turn the fish over and cook until browned on the second side and opaque in the center, 3 to 4 minutes longer. Transfer the swordfish steaks to plates and spoon the tomato relish on top.

# Grilled Idaho Rainbow Trout
## with Toasted Almonds

*Rainbow trout is available all year-round. While the fish comes from aquaculture hatcheries throughout the country, the state of Idaho is a major source of farm-raised trout. The boneless fillets called for in this recipe are marketed at 8 ounces dressed weight. Rainbow trout is offered on many restaurant menus, especially in tourist areas such as Sun Valley, where I had a delicious boned and grilled version. Trout is quite delicate and has a tendency to stick, so be sure to coat the grill pan with nonstick cooking spray before you heat it.*

*Makes 4 servings*

---

2 tablespoons unsalted butter
½ cup sliced blanched almonds
4 (8-ounce) skinless, boneless rainbow
    trout halves

1 tablespoon olive oil
¼ teaspoon salt
⅛ teaspoon freshly ground pepper
Fresh lemon wedges and parsley sprigs

---

**1.** In a small skillet, melt the butter over medium heat. Add the almonds and cook, stirring constantly, until they turn light brown. Immediately remove the almonds to a small bowl.

**2.** Brush the trout on both sides with the olive oil and season with the salt and pepper. Coat a grill pan with nonstick cooking spray, then heat the pan over medium heat until hot enough to make a few drops of water sizzle. Lay the fish on the hot pan, pinkest sides down, and cook until brown grill marks appear on the bottom, 3 to 4 minutes. With a wide spatula, gently turn the trout over and cook until the fish is just opaque in the center, about 3 minutes. With 1 or 2 spatulas, gently lift the fish onto 4 plates. Spoon the toasted nuts equally over each fish and garnish the plates with lemon wedges and parsley sprigs.

# Tuna Steaks with Sun-Dried Tomatoes and Toasted Pine Nuts

*This Spanish-accented sauce goes well with pan-grilled tuna steaks. The meaty fish cooks quickly, so take care not to overcook, or it will be dry.*

*Makes 4 servings*

---

3 tablespoons pine nuts
2 tablespoons olive oil
½ medium onion, finely chopped
2 garlic cloves, finely chopped
½ cup chicken broth
10 oil-packed sun-dried tomato halves,
    thinly sliced

2 tablespoons balsamic vinegar
Dash of cayenne
2 tablespoons chopped parsley
⅛ teaspoon salt
⅛ teaspoon freshly ground pepper
4 (6-ounce) fresh tuna steaks, about
    ¾ inch thick

---

**1.** In a small dry skillet, cook the pine nuts over medium heat, shaking the pan often, until they are toasted and lightly browned. Immediately remove to a small dish.
**2.** In a small saucepan, heat 1 tablespoon of the olive oil over medium heat. Add the onion and garlic and cook, stirring, until the onion is softened, 3 to 4 minutes. Add the chicken broth, sun-dried tomatoes, vinegar, and cayenne. Bring to a boil. Cook, stirring, 3 minutes. Add the pine nuts, parsley, salt, and pepper.
**3.** Brush the tuna steaks with the remaining 1 tablespoon of oil and season lightly with salt and pepper. Coat a grill pan with nonstick cooking spray, then heat the pan over medium heat until hot enough to make a few drops of water sizzle. Put the fish on the hot pan and cook until brown grill marks appear on the bottom, 3 to 4 minutes. Turn the tuna over and cook the second side until the fish is just barely opaque inside, 2 to 3 minutes. Serve the tuna with the sauce spooned on top.

# Seared Scallops with Sweet Red Pepper Sauce and Corn

*Succulent sea scallops arranged on a pool of red sauce with a scattering of yellow corn make a striking presentation. Serve with crusty bread.*

*Makes 4 servings*

---

2 large red bell peppers, chopped
1 tablespoon sweet Hungarian paprika
1 teaspoon ground cumin
3 to 4 drops of Tabasco or other hot sauce
½ cup chicken broth

1 teaspoon salt
2 ears of yellow corn
16 large sea scallops (about 1½ pounds)
1 tablespoon olive oil
1 tablespoon butter
Parsley or cilantro sprigs

---

**1.** In a medium saucepan, combine the bell peppers, paprika, cumin, Tabasco, broth, and ½ teaspoon of the salt. Bring to a boil, reduce the heat to low, cover, and cook until the peppers are very soft, 10 to 12 minutes. Transfer to a blender or food processor and puree until smooth. Strain the puree through a sieve back into the saucepan, using a wooden spoon to push as much of the solids through as you can. The sauce should be about as thick as heavy cream. Thin with a little additional chicken broth or water, if necessary. Set aside or cover and refrigerate for up to 3 days.

**2.** In a large pot of boiling water, cook the corn until crisp-tender, 2 to 3 minutes. Cool under cold running water. Cut the kernels off the cobs and set aside.

**3.** Pat the scallops dry with paper towels. Brush with the olive oil. Season the scallops with the remaining ½ teaspoon salt. Coat a grill pan with nonstick cooking spray and heat over medium heat until hot enough to make a few drops of water sizzle. Put the scallops on the hot pan and cook until golden on the bottom and marked from the grill, 3 to 4 minutes. Turn the scallops over and cook the second side until opaque throughout, 2 to 3 minutes longer.

**4.** To serve, reheat the red pepper sauce over medium-low heat. Meanwhile, in a medium skillet, melt the butter over medium heat. Add the corn kernels and stir until coated with butter. Divide the sauce equally among 4 dinner plates. Arrange the scallops on the sauce in the center of each plate. Scatter one-fourth of the corn over each serving. Garnish with sprigs of parsley or cilantro.

# Scallops with Spinach and Curried Cream Sauce

*Friends will think you've become a professional chef when you present them with this beautiful plate of food. The grilled scallops are perched on a bed of tender green spinach and surrounded by a creamy yellow curry sauce.*

*Makes 4 servings*

2 tablespoons butter

2 tablespoons flour

1 tablespoon imported Indian curry powder

1¼ cups whole milk (do not use low-fat or skim milk here)

Salt

1 (16-ounce) package prewashed baby spinach leaves

1 small garlic clove, crushed through a press

1½ tablespoons olive oil

Freshly ground pepper

16 large sea scallops (about 1½ pounds)

**1.** Melt the butter in a heavy medium saucepan over medium heat. Add the flour and cook, stirring, for 1 minute. Stir in the curry powder and continue to cook, stirring, for 30 to 45 seconds. Remove the pan from the heat and add the milk all at once. Whisk briskly to blend the milk with the roux. Return the pan to the heat. Cook, stirring, until the sauce comes to a boil. Reduce the heat to low and simmer until the sauce is smooth and thick, about 3 minutes. Season with salt to taste, remove from the heat, and set aside.

**2.** In a large pot of boiling water, or in a steaming basket over boiling water, cook the spinach until wilted and tender, 2 to 3 minutes. Drain the spinach very well, pressing to remove as much moisture as possible. Toss with the garlic and ½ tablespoon of the olive oil. Season with salt and pepper to taste.

**3.** Pat the scallops dry with paper towels and brush all over with the remaining 1 tablespoon of oil. Season the scallops lightly with salt. Coat a grill pan with nonstick cooking spray, then heat over medium heat until hot enough to make a few drops of water sizzle. Put the scallops on the hot pan and cook until golden brown on the bottom and marked from the grill, 3 to 4 minutes. Turn the scallops over and cook until the second side is browned and the scallops are opaque throughout, 2 to 3 minutes.

**4.** Reheat the curry sauce. Mound one-fourth of the warm spinach in the center of each of 4 large plates. Spoon the sauce around each mound of spinach. Arrange the grilled scallops on top and serve.

# Speedy Calamari Steaks

*Some fish markets carry perfectly formed pounded calamari steaks, which are delicious and worth looking for. It's hard to imagine anything simpler to prepare on the grill pan. From pan to plate in less than two minutes!*

*Makes 4 servings*

---

8 (3- to 4-ounce) pan-ready calamari
   steaks
1 tablespoon vegetable oil

¼ teaspoon salt
⅛ teaspoon freshly ground pepper
Fresh lemon wedges and parsley sprigs

---

**1.** Put the calamari steaks on a plate, and blot with paper towels to remove excess moisture. With your hands, rub the oil all over the calamari. Season with the salt and pepper.

**2.** Heat a grill pan over medium heat until hot enough to make a few drops of water sizzle. To insure that the calamari steaks cook quickly and do not steam and toughen, cook them in batches of 2 or 3. Put the calamari on the heated pan and cook until brown grill marks appear, 35 to 40 seconds. Turn over and cook for 30 to 35 seconds. Repeat until all the calamari steaks are cooked. Serve with lemon wedges to squeeze over the steaks and parsley as garnish.

# Grilled Mussels with Lemon Butter

*You'll need small plates and plenty of napkins to keep the juices off your chin when enjoying these little morsels. Accompany them with a fresh crusty baguette loaf to dip into the butter along with the mussels.*

*Makes 4 servings*

---

2 pounds small mussels, scrubbed and beards removed

2 teaspoons chopped fresh oregano or 1 teaspoon dried

4 tablespoons butter

1 garlic clove, crushed through a press

2 tablespoons fresh lemon juice

---

**1.** Heat a grill pan over medium heat until hot enough to make a few drops of water sizzle. Put the mussels in a single layer on the hot pan and sprinkle the oregano over them. Cover with a large sheet of aluminum foil or a dome lid and cook until all the mussels open, 4 to 5 minutes. Transfer the mussels to a warmed shallow bowl. Discard any mussels that do not open. Cover with the foil to keep warm.

**2.** In a small saucepan, melt the butter with the garlic over medium heat. Stir in the lemon juice. Put the lemon butter in a small bowl and serve with the mussels for dipping.

# Spicy Peanut Shrimp

*Indonesian-inspired peanut sauce, a sweet-hot combination, provides a tantalizing foil for America's most popular shellfish. I serve this over steamed rice with a generous sprinkling of chopped peanuts and cilantro and lime wedges to add icing to the cake.*

*Makes 4 servings*

---

1½ pounds large shrimp
¼ cup molasses
¼ cup smooth peanut butter
1 garlic clove, chopped
2 tablespoons Worcestershire sauce
1 tablespoon red wine vinegar
1 teaspoon chili powder

½ teaspoon salt
¼ teaspoon dried oregano
¼ teaspoon cayenne
Hot steamed rice, as accompaniment
¼ cup chopped roasted peanuts
2 tablespoons chopped cilantro
4 lime wedges

---

**1.** Shell and devein the shrimp, leaving the tails intact. Put the shrimp in a large bowl. In a blender or small food processor, combine the molasses, peanut butter, garlic, Worcestershire, vinegar, chili powder, salt, oregano, and cayenne. Add to the shrimp and stir well to coat. Cover and refrigerate for 45 to 50 minutes.

**2.** Heat a grill pan over medium heat until hot enough to make a few drops of water sizzle. Put the shrimp on the hot pan and cook, turning once, until pink and curled, 2 to 3 minutes per side. Serve the shrimp while hot over steamed rice. Sprinkle each serving with chopped peanuts and cilantro. Garnish with lime wedges.

# Sweet-and-Sour Pineapple Shrimp

*Almost everyone likes sweet-and-sour sauce. This version goes especially well with grilled shrimp. Serve the shrimp and the sauce over steamed white rice.*

*Makes 4 servings*

---

2½ tablespoons brown sugar

2 teaspoons cornstarch

½ teaspoon salt

½ cup chicken broth

2 tablespoons tomato ketchup

1 tablespoon rice vinegar

1 teaspoon soy sauce

1 (8-ounce) can pineapple chunks in juice

1 tablespoon vegetable oil

½ large white onion, sliced

½ red bell pepper, cut into ½-inch pieces

½ green bell pepper, cut into ½-inch pieces

1 pound large shrimp, shelled and deveined

---

**1.** In a medium bowl, mix the brown sugar, cornstarch, and salt. Stir in the chicken broth, ketchup, vinegar, and soy sauce. Drain the pineapple juice into the bowl with the cornstarch mixture. Stir well to blend. Set the sauce aside.

**2.** In a large nonstick skillet, heat the oil over medium heat. Add the onion and bell peppers. Cook until the vegetables are crisp-tender, 2 to 3 minutes. Add the cornstarch mixture. Cook, stirring, until the sauce thickens and clears, about 2 minutes. Add the pineapple chunks. Stir to combine. Remove from the heat and set aside.

**3.** Coat a grill pan with nonstick cooking spray, then heat the pan over medium heat until hot enough to make a few drops of water sizzle. Lay the shrimp on the hot pan and cook, turning 2 or 3 times, until the shrimp are pink and curled, 4 to 5 minutes.

**4.** Transfer the grilled shrimp to the skillet with the sweet-sour sauce. Stir gently to combine with the other ingredients. Heat through and serve.

# Tiger Shrimp with Sweet Pepper Sauce

*Giant tiger shrimp take well to the grill pan. For simplicity here, I use jarred roasted red peppers available in supermarkets. The shrimp and sauce are excellent over pasta or rice.*

*Makes 4 servings*

---

3 tablespoons olive oil
¼ cup finely chopped onion
2 garlic cloves, thinly sliced
1 cup drained chopped roasted red peppers
2 plum tomatoes, peeled, seeded, and chopped

1 teaspoon chili powder
¼ teaspoon salt
¼ teaspoon freshly ground pepper
16 tiger shrimp or other giant shrimp, peeled and deveined
¼ cup slivered fresh basil

---

**1.** In a medium saucepan, heat 1½ tablespoons of the olive oil over medium heat. Add the onion and garlic. Cook, stirring, until the onion and garlic soften and begin to color, 3 to 4 minutes. Add the roasted peppers, tomatoes, chili powder, salt, and pepper. Bring to a boil, reduce the heat to low, cover, and simmer, stirring frequently, for about 5 minutes to blend the flavors. Transfer the mixture to a food processor and puree until smooth. Return the pepper sauce to the same pan. Cover and cook over low heat for 5 minutes. Season with additional salt and pepper to taste.

**2.** Put the shrimp into a large bowl. Add the remaining 1½ tablespoons olive oil and toss to coat the shrimp with oil. Season the shrimp lightly with additional salt and pepper and toss again. Heat a grill pan over medium heat until hot enough to make a few drops of water sizzle. Put the shrimp on the hot pan and cook, turning 3 to 4 times, until the shrimp are marked from the grill on both sides and opaque throughout, about 8 minutes total. Reheat the sauce and serve with the shrimp. Sprinkle the basil over the top.

# Chapter Four
# Grilled Chicken and Meats

Here's where the grill pan really shines. Cooking chicken and other meats on the grill pan is a light way of cooking with less fat. Plus there's the bonus of that smoky smell and taste, and professional grilled look, which simulates an outdoor barbecue.

The best cuts of meat or chicken to cook on the grill pan are those on the thin side; about ½ to 1 inch thick is ideal. (For larger pieces and thick cuts, see Chapter Five, page 140.) Pieces should be uniform in size and weight for even cooking. Here are over two dozen tempting recipes for grilled chicken and meats. Some of the recipes, such as Grilled Garlic Chicken with Couscous, Pecans, and Raisins or Lamb Strips with Lentils, make a complete meal on the plate. With others that just deal with the meat, such as Chicken Breasts with Orange-Thyme Sauce, Lamb Steaks with Sweet Peppers and Onions, or Duck Breasts with Warm Cranberry Vinaigrette, I've suggested appropriate accompaniments to serve with the dish.

# Chicken Breasts with Orange-Thyme Sauce

*The sweet-tart sauce here can be prepared ahead and reheated, which makes this quick elegant presentation perfect for company. Serve with wild rice or orzo and buttered broccoli.*

*Makes 4 servings*

---

1 tablespoon butter

1 tablespoon vegetable oil

⅓ cup finely chopped onion

2 garlic cloves, finely chopped

¼ teaspoon dried thyme

2 tablespoons dry vermouth

2 tablespoons frozen orange juice concentrate, undiluted

2 teaspoons honey

1 teaspoon cider vinegar

½ cup chicken broth

1 teaspoon cornstarch

1 teaspoon fresh lemon juice

Salt and freshly ground pepper

4 skinless, boneless chicken breast halves

---

**1.** In a small saucepan, melt the butter in the oil over medium heat. Add the onion, garlic, and thyme. Cook, stirring, until the onion softens and begins to brown, 3 to 5 minutes. Stir in the vermouth, orange juice concentrate, honey, and vinegar. Bring to a boil, reduce the heat to low, and cook until the sauce is thickened and sticky, 3 to 4 minutes.

**2.** In a cup, stir together the cold chicken broth and cornstarch until blended. Whisk into the sauce in the saucepan. Cook, stirring, until the sauce boils and thickens, 1 to 2 minutes. Stir in the lemon juice, and season to taste with salt and pepper. Remove from the heat and set aside.

**3.** Season the chicken breasts with salt and pepper. Heat a grill pan over medium heat until hot enough to make a few drops of water sizzle. Put the chicken breasts on the heated pan. Cook until the top edges of the chicken are opaque and brown grill marks appear on the bottom, 4 to 5 minutes. Turn the chicken over and cook the second side until the meat is no longer pink in the thickest part, another 3 to 4 minutes.

**4.** Reheat the sauce over low heat until warm. Serve the chicken with 1 tablespoon of the sauce spooned over each piece. Pass the remainder at the table.

# Grilled Garlic Chicken with Couscous, Pecans, and Raisins

*Just about everyone loves couscous with chicken, and cooks everywhere will love to serve this palate-pleasing combination. Add a green salad for a complete meal.*

*Makes 4 servings*

---

4 skinless, boneless chicken breast halves
1 garlic clove, crushed through a press
3 tablespoons extra-virgin olive oil
1 teaspoon salt
1 (10-ounce) package plain couscous
½ cup coarsely chopped pecans

¼ cup raisins
2 scallions, finely chopped
1 teaspoon ground cumin
2 teaspoons fresh lemon juice
1 tablespoon chopped parsley
⅛ teaspoon freshly ground pepper

---

**1.** Put the chicken breasts between 2 sheets of plastic wrap and pound with the flat side of a wooden mallet or a rolling pin to an even thickness of about ½ inch. Rub the breasts with the garlic, 1 tablespoon of the olive oil, and ½ teaspoon of the salt. Put the chicken breasts on a plate and set aside.

**2.** In a medium saucepan, bring 2¼ cups water, the remaining ½ teaspoon salt, and 1 tablespoon of the olive oil to a boil. Add the couscous and stir well. Cover and remove from the heat. Let stand while cooking the chicken.

**3.** Heat a grill pan over medium heat until hot enough to make a few drops of water sizzle. Lay the chicken breasts, smooth sides down, on the pan and cook until brown grill marks appear on the bottom, 5 to 6 minutes. Turn the chicken over and cook until the second side is browned and the chicken is white in the center but still juicy, 3 to 4 minutes. Remove the breasts to a cutting board, cover with foil to keep warm, and let stand 3 to 4 minutes.

---

**4.** Meanwhile, fluff the couscous with a fork and gently stir in the remaining 1 tablespoon oil, the pecans, raisins, scallions, cumin, lemon juice, parsley, and pepper. Divide the couscous evenly among 4 heated plates. Slice the chicken breasts crosswise, arrange on the couscous, and serve.

# Chicken Breasts with Mexican Red Chili-Citrus Sauce

*This full-flavored Mexican sauce sparks up simple grilled chicken beautifully. Dried ancho chiles can be found in the Mexican ingredients section of most supermarkets.*

*Makes 6 servings*

---

4 ancho chiles
2 tablespoons plus 2 teaspoons vegetable oil
3 shallots, finely chopped
2 garlic cloves, thinly sliced
1 teaspoon dried oregano, preferably Mexican
¾ cup chicken broth
½ cup dry, full-bodied red wine, such as zinfandel or burgundy
3 tablespoons undiluted frozen orange juice concentrate, thawed
1 tablespoon rice vinegar
2 tablespoons tomato paste
1 tablespoon dark brown sugar
1 teaspoon salt
6 skinless, boneless chicken breast halves
Cilantro or parsley sprigs

---

**1.** Wipe the anchos with a damp paper towel if they are dusty. Using scissors, cut the chiles open and remove the stems and seeds. Heat a grill pan over medium heat until hot enough to make a few drops of water sizzle and toast the chiles, turning, until they are aromatic, 1 to 2 minutes. Do not burn, or the chiles will be bitter.

**2.** Bring a medium saucepan of water to a boil. Add the toasted chiles, pushing them down into the water. Cover the pan, remove from the heat, and soak the chiles for 20 to 30 minutes to soften.

**3.** Meanwhile, in a medium skillet, heat 2 tablespoons of the oil over medium heat. Add the shallots, garlic, and oregano. Cook, stirring, until the shallots are just beginning to brown, 2 to 3 minutes. Add the broth, wine, orange juice concentrate, vinegar, tomato paste, brown sugar, and ½ teaspoon of the salt. Bring to a boil, reduce the heat to low, and simmer, stirring frequently, for 5 minutes.

**4.** Scrape the skillet contents into a blender or food processor. Lift the chiles from the soaking liquid and add to the blender. Puree until smooth. The sauce should be about as thick as ketchup. If too thick, add water or additional chicken broth, 1 tablespoon at a time, to achieve the desired consistency. Place a wire strainer over a medium saucepan and strain the sauce into the pan. Press the soft pulp through with a wooden spoon. Discard any remaining bits of skin. Bring the sauce to a boil over medium heat, reduce the heat to low, and cook, stirring frequently, for 6 to 8 minutes to blend the flavors. Remove the sauce from the heat, cover, and set aside. (The sauce can be made ahead to this point up to a day ahead and reheated shortly before serving.)

**5.** Brush the chicken with the remaining 2 teaspoons oil. Season with the remaining ½ teaspoon salt. Heat a grill pan over medium heat until hot enough to make a few drops of water sizzle. Put the chicken on the heated pan and cook until grill marks appear on the bottom, 4 to 5 minutes. Turn the breasts over and cook the second side until the chicken is white in the center but still juicy, another 4 to 5 minutes.

**6.** To serve, reheat the sauce. Spoon a pool of sauce onto each serving plate. Cut each chicken breast crosswise into 1½-inch strips and arrange, overlapping, on the sauce. Garnish with cilantro or parsley sprigs.

# Chicken Kebabs

*Indian spices add interest to these kebabs while yogurt tenderizes the chicken in this skewered version of tandoori chicken. Serve the kebabs over a bed of steamed basmati rice, with chutney on the side.*

*Makes 4 servings*

---

4 skinless, boneless chicken breast halves
½ cup plain yogurt
1 tablespoon minced garlic
½ tablespoon imported Indian curry
   powder

1 tablespoon crushed dried mint
½ teaspoon salt
¼ teaspoon freshly ground pepper
⅛ teaspoon cayenne, or to taste
Vegetable oil

---

**1.** Trim any excess fat from the chicken. Cut the breasts into 1-inch pieces. In a large bowl, mix together the yogurt, garlic, curry powder, mint, salt, black pepper, and cayenne. Add the chicken and stir to coat. Cover and refrigerate 6 hours or overnight, if possible.

**2.** Loosely thread the chicken on thick wooden skewers. Heat a grill pan over medium heat until hot enough to make a few drops of water sizzle. Brush the pan with oil. Put the kebabs on the heated pan, and cook, turning 3 or 4 times, or as necessary for even cooking, until lightly browned and the chicken is white throughout but still juicy, 8 to 10 minutes.

# Chicken Breasts with Italian Salsa Verde

*The piquant, herb-flecked Italian sauce that accompanies the chicken here can be prepared up to 3 hours in advance. Be sure to use your best extra-virgin olive oil for this dish and don't skimp on the parsley.*

*Makes 4 servings*

---

½ cup loosely packed flat-leaf parsley

2 tablespoons chopped fresh mint

3 tablespoons fresh lemon juice

1½ teaspoons chopped shallot

1 teaspoon anchovy paste

1 or 2 garlic cloves, coarsely chopped

¼ cup plus 1 teaspoon extra-virgin olive oil

1 tablespoon drained capers

½ teaspoon salt

¼ teaspoon freshly ground pepper

4 skinless, boneless chicken breast halves

---

**1.** In a food processor or blender, combine the parsley, mint, lemon juice, shallot, anchovy paste, garlic, and ¼ cup of the olive oil. Puree until the herbs are minced. Transfer the sauce to a small nonreactive bowl. Stir in the capers. Season to taste with salt and pepper. (The sauce may not need salt at all because both the anchovy paste and capers are salty.) Cover and set aside until ready to serve.

**2.** Trim any excess fat from the chicken breasts. Place each breast between two sheets of plastic wrap and pound lightly to an even thickness of about ½ inch. Brush the chicken with the remaining 1 teaspoon oil. Season with the salt and pepper.

**3.** Heat a grill pan over medium heat until hot enough to make a few drops of water sizzle. Put the chicken breasts, smooth sides down, on the pan. Cook until brown grill marks appear on the bottom of the chicken, 4 to 5 minutes. Turn the breasts over. Cook until the meat is white throughout but still juicy, 3 to 4 minutes. Spoon half of the salsa verde over the chicken. Pass the remaining sauce on the side.

# Sweet-and-Sour Grilled Chicken
# with Roasted Cashews

*Packaged chicken tenders are exceptionally convenient and an excellent choice for this popular Chinese-style chicken dish. Serve with steamed rice.*

*Makes 4 servings*

2 tablespoons packed brown sugar

2 teaspoons cornstarch

½ teaspoon salt

½ cup reduced-sodium canned chicken broth

2 tablespoons ketchup

2 tablespoons soy sauce

1 tablespoon rice vinegar

⅛ teaspoon crushed hot red pepper

2 tablespoons vegetable oil

1 medium green bell pepper, cut into strips about ½ inch wide

1 celery rib, cut crosswise into ½-inch pieces

1 medium white onion, sliced

¾ pound chicken breast tenders

1 large ripe tomato, cut into ¾-inch pieces

½ cup whole roasted cashews

**1.** In a small bowl, mix the brown sugar, cornstarch, and salt. Stir in the chicken broth, ketchup, soy sauce, vinegar, and hot pepper. Set the sauce aside.

**2.** In a large nonstick skillet, heat 1 tablespoon of the oil over medium heat. Add the bell pepper, celery, and onion. Cook, stirring, until the vegetables are crisp-tender, 2 to 3 minutes. Add the cornstarch mixture. Cook, stirring, until the sauce thickens and clears, about 2 minutes. Set aside in the pan.

**3.** Put the chicken tenders in a bowl. Add the remaining 1 tablespoon of oil and toss to coat. Heat a grill pan over medium heat until hot enough to make a few drops of water sizzle. Put the chicken tenders on the heated pan and cook, turning 2 or 3 times, until the chicken tenders are light brown on the outside and white on the inside but still juicy, 3 to 4 minutes.

**4.** Put the tenders into the skillet with the sweet-sour sauce, and stir gently to combine with the other ingredients. Add the tomato and the roasted cashews at the last minute.

# Chicken, Pork, and Apple Sausage Patties

*Using a food processor, homemade sausages are easy to make and a tremendous treat. These fresh sausages are lean, mild, and really versatile. Try the patties for breakfast or brunch with omelets, or put them on a bun as a sausage burger for lunch, or serve them for dinner with mashed potatoes and creamed corn. Note that the sausage patties are made ahead to allow time for the spices to develop.*

*Makes 8 patties*

---

½ pound skinless, boneless chicken thigh meat
½ pound fresh ground pork
1 small green Pippin or Granny Smith apple, peeled, cored, and coarsely chopped
1 tablespoon brandy

2 teaspoons maple syrup
1 teaspoon salt
½ teaspoon dried thyme
¼ teaspoon ground allspice
¼ teaspoon freshly ground pepper
¼ teaspoon crushed hot red pepper
1½ tablespoons vegetable oil

---

**1.** Cut the chicken into 1-inch chunks. Put in a food processor. Add all the remaining ingredients except the oil and pulse several times. Scrape down the sides of the bowl and pulse until the chicken is ground to a medium-coarse texture. Do not overprocess to a paste. Form the sausage into 8 patties about ½ inch thick. Put the patties on a plate, cover, and refrigerate 4 to 6 hours or overnight.

**2.** Coat a grill pan with nonstick cooking spray, then heat the pan over medium heat until hot enough to make a few drops of water sizzle. Brush the sausage patties lightly with the oil and put them on the hot pan. Cook, turning 2 or 3 times, until the patties are brown outside and no longer pink inside, 6 to 8 minutes total. Serve while hot.

# Jalapeño Jelly-Glazed Turkey Cutlets

*A zesty jalapeño pepper jelly glaze adds color and extra flavor to turn this low-fat turkey dish into something special. After brushing the turkey with the jelly, turn the cutlets frequently for more even browning and to prevent burning. The cooking time will vary depending on the thickness of the cutlets. Serve with rice and baked acorn squash.*

*Makes 4 servings*

---

¼ cup red jalapeño jelly

1 tablespoon fresh lemon juice

1 teaspoon chili powder

4 turkey cutlets (6 to 7 ounces each)

2 teaspoons vegetable oil

½ teaspoon salt

---

**1.** In a small saucepan, heat the jelly with 2 teaspoons of water over medium heat, stirring as it melts. Mix in the lemon juice and chili powder. Set the glaze aside.

**2.** Brush the turkey on both sides with the vegetable oil. Season with the salt. Heat a grill pan over medium heat until hot enough to make a few drops of water sizzle. Put the turkey cutlets on the hot pan and cook until brown grill marks appear on the bottom, 2 to 3 minutes. Brush the tops of the cutlets with a thin coat of the jalapeño jelly glaze and turn the turkey over. Brush the tops of the cutlets with glaze and continue cooking, turning the cutlets and basting them with glaze frequently, until very brown and cooked through, 3 to 4 minutes.

**3.** Arrange the cutlets on a plate. Bring the remaining glaze to a boil and cook for 1 minute. Transfer to a small serving bowl to pass on the side.

# Turkey Jalapeño Patties

*Jalapeño peppers vary wildly in degree of heat; they can be mild or wild. The best way to get some indication of the heat level is to cut them open and take a whiff. There's a stinging pungency in the hottest ones. If you want to tame the heat, remove the seeds and the white veins or "ribs," where the heat lurks, and chop the rest. If you prefer your food really hot, leave the veins intact. For the patties, buy ground turkey that is a mixture of dark and white meat. All white meat ground turkey is too dry for this recipe.*

*Makes 4 servings*

---

1 pound ground turkey
⅓ cup fine dry bread crumbs
2 tablespoons dry vermouth
2 scallions, finely chopped

1 large fresh jalapeño pepper, seeded
  and finely chopped
½ teaspoon salt
⅛ teaspoon freshly ground pepper

---

**1.** In a medium bowl, combine all of the ingredients. Mix very well. Form the meat into 8 patties about 3 inches across and ½ inch thick.

**2.** Heat a grill pan over medium heat until hot enough to make a few drops of water sizzle. Put the patties on the hot pan and press lightly with a wide spatula to be sure the meat makes contact with the grill. Cook the patties until brown grill marks appear on the bottom, 3 to 4 minutes. Turn the patties over and cook until brown on the second side and the meat is no longer pink inside, about 3 minutes longer.

# Duck Breasts with Warm Cranberry Vinaigrette

*When it's time to plan a holiday dinner, try boneless duck breasts with this light tart-sweet sauce. Garlic mashed potatoes go very well with this dish.*

*Makes 4 servings*

---

1 cup fresh cranberries, rinsed
3 tablespoons sugar
Zest and juice of 1 navel orange
1 tablespoon red wine vinegar
4 skinless, boneless duck breasts (6 to 7 ounces each)

1 teaspoon vegetable oil
½ teaspoon salt
¼ teaspoon freshly ground pepper

---

**1.** In a nonreactive saucepan, combine the cranberries, sugar, orange zest, orange juice, vinegar, and ½ cup water. Bring to a boil over medium heat. Cook, stirring, until the cranberries pop, about 5 minutes. Crush the berries with their juices. Remove from the heat and set aside, covered, to keep warm.

**2.** Brush the duck breasts with the oil. Season with the salt and pepper. Heat a grill pan over medium heat until hot enough to make a few drops of water sizzle. Put the breasts on the hot pan and cook until brown grill marks appear on the bottom, 5 to 6 minutes. Turn the breasts over and cook the second side until brown outside and pink inside, 4 to 5 minutes for medium-rare.

**3.** Transfer the duck to a cutting board. Let stand, loosely covered with foil, for 5 minutes, then slice thinly crosswise. To serve, arrange the duck slices on a platter. Rewarm the cranberry sauce and spoon over the duck.

# Cowboy T-Bone Steaks

*Here's a great way to get that cooked-outdoors flavor even though you're grilling the steaks indoors on the grill pan. An onion and green chile topping adds an exciting bite to the juicy steaks. Serve with corn on the cob or baked potatoes and a tossed salad.*

*Makes 4 servings*

---

2 tablespoons plus 2 teaspoons olive oil

2 medium onions, sliced

3 fresh poblano or Anaheim chiles, seeded and cut into thin strips

3 large garlic cloves, chopped

1 tablespoon chili powder

½ teaspoon dried oregano

1¼ teaspoons salt

½ teaspoon freshly ground pepper

4 (8-ounce) T-bone steaks, about ¾ inch thick, trimmed of excess fat

---

**1.** In a large skillet, heat 2 tablespoons of the olive oil over medium heat. Add the onions and cook, stirring frequently, until the onions begin to brown, 4 to 5 minutes. Add the poblano strips, garlic, chili powder, and oregano. Stir in 3 tablespoons water. Cover the skillet, reduce the heat to low, and cook until the liquid is absorbed, about 3 minutes. Season with ¼ teaspoon of the salt and set the onion-chile topping aside.

**2.** Brush the steaks with the remaining 2 teaspoons olive oil and season with the remaining 1 teaspoon salt and the pepper. Heat a grill pan (preferably double-burner) over medium heat until hot enough to make a few drops of water sizzle. Put the steaks on the hot pan and cook until brown grill marks appear on the bottom, 4 to 5 minutes. (If using a smaller grill pan, cook the steaks 2 at a time.) Turn the steaks over and cook the second side to the desired doneness, about 3 to 4 minutes for medium-rare. Spoon the onion-chile topping over the steaks and serve at once.

# New York Strip Steak

*An excellent steak needs only salt and pepper and careful grilling to make the most of its juicy succulence. A New York strip steak is one of my top choices when I'm in a steak mood, and the stove-top grill pan does it exactly to my liking.*

*Makes 4 servings*

---

4 (6-ounce) New York strip steaks, cut
   ¾ inch thick
2 teaspoons vegetable oil

½ teaspoon salt
¼ teaspoon freshly ground pepper

---

Trim the fat from the steaks. Brush both sides with the vegetable oil. Season with the salt and pepper. Heat a grill pan over medium heat until hot enough to make a few drops of water sizzle. Put the steaks on the hot pan and cook until brown grill marks appear on the bottom, 2 to 3 minutes. Turn the steaks over and cook the second side for 2 to 3 minutes. Turn the steaks once more, reposition them on the raised grids to achieve a cross-hatched pattern, and cook for 2 to 3 minutes for rare or to the desired degree of doneness. Serve at once.

# Tequila-Lime Flank Steak with Pickled Red Onions

*Plan a fiesta around this Mexican-inspired steak. Start with margaritas, guacamole, and tortilla chips. Pair the steak with Mexican rice and beans and a shredded carrot and jicama salad dressed with lime vinaigrette.*

*Makes 8 servings*

---

2 beef flank steaks (about 1½ pounds each), trimmed of fat and membrane

3 garlic cloves, minced

½ teaspoon freshly ground pepper

⅓ cup tequila

3 tablespoons fresh lime juice

1 tablespoon honey

¼ teaspoon bottled Maggi seasoning extract

3 tablespoons plus 1 teaspoon vegetable oil

1½ teaspoons salt

Pickled Red Onions (recipe follows on page 122)

---

**1.** With a sharp knife, score the steak on both sides in a diamond pattern ⅛ to ¼ inch deep. Rub the meat all over with the garlic and pepper. Place the steaks in a shallow glass baking dish.

**2.** In a small bowl, mix the tequila, lime juice, honey, and Maggi seasoning. Whisk in 3 tablespoons of the oil. Drizzle 2 tablespoons of the marinade over each steak; reserve the remainder. Turn the meat over 2 or 3 times to distribute the marinade. Cover and refrigerate for about 1 hour or for up to 8 hours. Remove the meat from the refrigerator 30 to 60 minutes before cooking. Pat dry with paper towels. Season the steaks with the salt just before grilling.

**3.** Brush a grill pan with the remaining 1 teaspoon of oil and heat over medium heat until hot enough to make a few drops of water sizzle. Put 1 steak on the hot pan and cook until brown grill marks appear on the bottom, 6 to 8 minutes. Brush lightly with the reserved marinade and turn over. Cook the second side another 5 to 6 minutes for medium-rare. Repeat with the remaining oil, steak, and marinade.

**4.** Remove the steaks to a cutting board and let stand about 5 minutes. Cut across the grain into thin slices. Serve with Pickled Red Onions.

# Pickled Red Onions

*Makes about ¾ cup*

---

3 tablespoons olive oil
1 large red onion, quartered and thinly
  sliced
½ teaspoon dried oregano, preferably
  Mexican

1 to 2 tablespoons red wine vinegar
½ teaspoon sugar
⅛ teaspoon salt
⅛ teaspoon freshly ground pepper

---

**1.** In a medium skillet, heat the olive oil over medium heat. Add the red onion and oregano. Cook, stirring, until the onion is barely tender, 2 to 3 minutes. Transfer to a bowl.

**2.** Stir in the vinegar and sugar. Season with the salt and pepper. Marinate at room temperature for at least 1 hour or refrigerate overnight. Serve at room temperature or sizzle briefly in a hot skillet just before serving.

# Marinated Filet Mignon Milano

*Indulge with steaks special enough for a celebration. The lean tender steaks are given a special flavor by resting in a balsamic marinade before sizzling on the grill to a rich brown.*

*Makes 4 servings*

---

2 tablespoons olive oil
1 tablespoon balsamic vinegar
1 large garlic clove, crushed through a
    press
¼ teaspoon dried thyme

4 (6- to 7-ounce) filet mignon steaks,
    cut 1 to 1½ inches thick
½ teaspoon salt
¼ teaspoon freshly ground pepper

---

**1.** In a small bowl, whisk together the olive oil, vinegar, garlic, and thyme. Put the steaks in a 1-quart self-sealing plastic bag. Pour in the marinade. Turn 3 or 4 times to coat the steaks with the marinade. Refrigerate 3 to 4 hours. Remove the steaks from the refrigerator about 1 hour before cooking.

**2.** Remove the steaks from the marinade and pat the meat dry. Season with the salt and pepper. Heat a grill pan over medium heat until hot enough to make a few drops of water sizzle. Lay the steaks on the hot pan and cook until medium-rare, 5 to 6 minutes on each side. Serve at once.

# Thai Basil Beef

*In my version of this popular Thai restaurant item, the beef is cooked on a stove-top grill pan instead of being stir-fried. The sauce ingredients starred with asterisks can be found in Asian specialty markets or in the Asian foods section of many supermarkets. Serve with steamed rice.*

*Makes 4 servings*

---

1 tablespoon vegetable oil

2 tablespoons Thai or Vietnamese fish sauce (nam pla or nuoc mam)*

1 tablespoon Chinese oyster sauce*

2 teaspoons soy sauce

½ teaspoon Chinese chili paste with garlic

1 garlic clove, minced

1 tablespoon sugar

½ cup chicken broth

1 (1-pound) beef flank steak, cut across the grain on the diagonal into ¼-inch-thick slices

1 cup lightly packed, coarsely shredded fresh basil

2 teaspoons fresh lime juice

---

**1.** In a medium skillet, heat 1 teaspoon of the vegetable oil over medium heat. Add the fish sauce, oyster sauce, soy sauce, chili sauce, garlic, and sugar. Cook, stirring, until the mixture boils and the sugar melts, about 1 minute. Add the chicken broth, and bring to a boil, stirring. Cook for 1 minute. Remove the pan from the heat and set the sauce aside.

**2.** Brush the beef slices with the remaining 2 teaspoons oil. Heat a grill pan over medium heat until hot enough to make a few drops of water sizzle. Put the beef slices on the hot pan and cook, turning once, until the slices are lightly browned but still pink in the center, 4 to 5 minutes total. Transfer the beef to a cutting board and cut the slices crosswise into 2-inch pieces.

**3.** Add the grilled beef to the skillet with the sauce. Add the basil and lime juice. Bring to a boil, turning the meat over once or twice, until heated through, about 1 minute.

# Grilled Beef Steak, Poblano Peppers, and Tomatoes over Pasta

*Makes 4 servings*

---

1 (1- to 1¼-pound) flank steak
½ teaspoon vegetable oil
1 garlic clove, finely chopped
½ teaspoon dried oregano
¾ teaspoon salt
½ teaspoon freshly ground pepper
2 large poblano peppers

1 pound penne pasta
¼ cup extra-virgin olive oil
3 ripe medium tomatoes, peeled and
  coarsely chopped
⅓ cup chopped pitted kalamata olives
¼ cup loosely packed slivered fresh basil

---

**1.** Trim the silvery membrane and any excess fat from the flank steak. With a large sharp knife, score the steak on both sides in a diamond pattern ⅛ to ¼ inch deep. Put the steak on a platter and rub all over with the oil, garlic, and oregano. Season with ¼ teaspoon each salt and pepper. Cut the seasoned steak crosswise on a diagonal into thin strips. Put the steak strips on a plate and set aside.

**2.** Roast the poblanos directly over a gas flame or under a broiler until charred all over. Put the charred peppers into a plastic bag and let steam for about 10 minutes. Rub the skins off the peppers and remove the stems and seeds. Rinse the peppers and cut into thin strips about ¼ inch wide. Put the pepper strips into a bowl and reserve.

**3.** In a large pot of boiling salted water, cook the pasta until tender but still firm, 10 to 12 minutes; drain, but do not rinse. Return the hot pasta to the cooking pot. Add the olive oil, tomatoes, chopped olives, reserved pepper strips, and the remaining ½ teaspoon salt and ¼ teaspoon pepper. Toss well to combine the ingredients. Cover the pot and set aside.

**4.** Heat a grill pan over medium heat until hot enough to make a few drops of water sizzle. Put the steak strips on the hot pan and cook, turning 2 or 3 times, until the strips are brown on both sides and barely pink inside, about 5 minutes total. Put the steak strips on a cutting board and cut crosswise into bite-sized pieces. Add the steak pieces to the pasta, and toss to combine. To serve, divide the pasta equally among 4 serving plates. Scatter the basil on top.

# London Broil

*London broil, a thick, lean, boneless cut of beef, such as top round, has long been a favorite of barbecue fans. Marinate the steak overnight in the refrigerator to intensify the flavor.*

*Makes 4 to 6 servings*

1 (1½-pound) London broil steak, about 1¼ inches thick
2 tablespoons olive oil
2 tablespoons red wine vinegar
1 tablespoon fresh lemon juice
1 teaspoon Worcestershire sauce

1 shallot, chopped
2 garlic cloves, crushed through a press
1 teaspoon dried oregano
½ teaspoon freshly ground pepper
1 teaspoon salt

**1.** Put the steak in a large shallow glass baking dish. In a small bowl, mix together the olive oil, vinegar, lemon juice, Worcestershire, shallot, garlic, oregano, and pepper. Pour the marinade over the meat and turn several times to coat. Cover and refrigerate at least 8 hours or overnight, turning the steak 2 or 3 times while it marinates.

**2.** Remove the meat from the marinade about 1 hour before grilling. Pat the meat dry with paper towels. Season on both sides with the salt.

**3.** Coat a grill pan with nonstick cooking spray, then heat over medium heat until hot enough to make a few drops of water sizzle. Put the meat on the hot pan and cook until brown grill marks appear on the bottom, 6 to 7 minutes. Turn the steak over and cook the second side another 6 minutes. Turn the meat again, reposition on the grids to achieve cross-hatched grill marks, and cook for 3 to 4 more minutes for medium-rare. Remove the meat to a cutting board and let stand for 5 minutes. To serve, cut the London broil across the grain into thin slices.

# Grilled Calf's Liver with Onion and Green Pepper

*Makes 4 servings*

1 pound calf's liver, trimmed and cut
    into 4 equal pieces
1 tablespoon olive oil
¼ teaspoon salt
⅛ teaspoon freshly ground pepper

2 strips of bacon
1 medium onion, sliced ⅜ inch thick
½ green bell pepper, sliced ⅜ inch
    thick

**1.** Brush the liver with the olive oil, and season with the salt and pepper. Set aside.
**2.** Heat a grill pan over medium heat until hot enough to make a few drops of water sizzle. Put the bacon strips on the hot pan and cook, turning 2 to 3 times, until lightly browned, 4 to 5 minutes. Remove the bacon and drain on paper towels. Cut the bacon crosswise into ¼-inch pieces and reserve.
**3.** Put the onion and bell pepper on the grill pan and cook, turning with tongs, until the vegetables are tender, 4 to 5 minutes. Remove the vegetables to a plate.
**4.** Put the liver on the hot pan and cook, turning 2 or 3 times, until the liver is brown on the outside and pink on the inside, 5 to 6 minutes total. Serve the liver with the onion, pepper, and bacon scattered over the top.

# Mustard-Seasoned Pork Chops

*Modern American pork is much leaner than in the past, and it's important not to overcook the pork, which causes it to toughen. These delicious chops are seasoned with Dijon mustard, olive oil, and herbs to add flavor and also to help keep the pork moist and tender.*

*Makes 4 servings*

---

1 tablespoon Dijon mustard
1 tablespoon olive oil
½ teaspoon dried oregano
¼ teaspoon dried thyme
1 garlic clove, finely chopped

¼ teaspoon salt
⅛ teaspoon freshly ground pepper
4 (6-ounce) loin pork chops, about
⅜ inch thick, trimmed of fat

---

**1.** In a small bowl, mix together the mustard, olive oil, oregano, thyme, garlic, salt, and pepper. Brush the pork chops all over with the mixture and let stand about 30 minutes.

**2.** Coat a grill pan with nonstick cooking spray, then heat the grill pan over medium heat until hot enough to make a few drops of water sizzle. Place the pork chops on the heated pan and cook, turning 2 or 3 times, until brown on the outside and no longer pink in the center, 10 to 12 minutes total.

# Korean Spicy Grilled Pork and Scallions

*Use lean pork from the loin sliced very thinly for this dish. Grill some scallions at the same time to serve with the pork. Crisp romaine lettuce leaves are a customary accompaniment in which to roll up the grilled pork and scallions.*

*Makes 4 servings*

---

1⅓ pounds lean boneless pork loin, sliced very thin

2½ tablespoons soy sauce

2 teaspoons sugar

2 teaspoons rice vinegar

3 garlic cloves, finely chopped

2 teaspoons grated fresh ginger

1 teaspoon Chinese chili paste with garlic

½ teaspoon Asian sesame oil

8 scallions, white and 2 inches of tender green only

Romaine lettuce leaves

---

**1.** Pound the pork slices lightly to an even thickness, if necessary. Put the meat into a glass pie plate. In a small bowl, combine the soy sauce, sugar, vinegar, garlic, ginger, chile paste, and sesame oil. Pour over the pork and turn the meat several times to coat with the marinade. Let stand at room temperature for 30 to 45 minutes.

**2.** Spray a grill pan with nonstick cooking spray, then heat over medium heat until hot enough to make a few drops of water sizzle. Put the seasoned meat on the hot pan in batches and cook, turning 2 or 3 times, until nicely browned and cooked through, 3 to 4 minutes per batch.

**3.** While the pork is cooking, lay the scallions on the outer edges of the grill pan. Cook them, turning once, until the scallions are limp and crisp-tender, 3 to 4 minutes. Pile the cooked pork on a serving plate. Arrange the scallions around the edge of the plate and serve with lettuce leaves on the side for wrappers.

# Country Ham Steak with Apple Rounds

*Ham is good eating around the clock. The flavor of fully cooked ham is enhanced by a brief stove-top browning on the grill pan. Ditto for the sweet apple rounds, which provide a fine companion to the ham.*

*Makes 4 servings*

---

2 or 3 tart-sweet red apples
2 fully cooked bone-in ham steaks
  (about 1 pound each)

2 tablespoons melted butter
1 to 2 teaspoons sugar

---

**1.** Rinse the apples and dry them with paper towels. Core the apples, leaving the skin on. Cut crosswise into ¼-inch-thick rounds.

**2.** Trim any excess fat from the ham. Heat a grill pan over medium heat until hot enough to make a few drops of water sizzle. Lay the ham on the hot pan and cook until brown grill marks appear on the bottom, 3 to 4 minutes. Turn the ham over and cook 2 minutes. Remove the ham to a warm platter and cover with foil to keep warm.

**3.** Brush the apples slices with the melted butter and lay them on the heated grill pan. Cook until lightly marked from the grill, 2 to 3 minutes. Turn and grill the second side until lightly marked, 1 to 2 minutes.

**4.** Sprinkle the tops of the apple rounds lightly with sugar. Turn the slices over again and cook 30 to 40 seconds to caramelize the sugar, but do not let it burn. Arrange the apples on the platter with the ham, and serve at once.

# Sausage and Red Onion Mixed Grill

*After a day of outdoor activity, you can satisfy big appetites by cooking a selection of sausages. These days, both gourmet butcher shops and deli meat counters offer quite a range of flavors. Grilled onions are a natural "go-with" for them. And both take beautifully to the stove-top grill pan, which is ready for instant action. For easy self-service, set out country bread, buns, and all the trimmings, along with a couple of salads, such as potato salad, bean salad, or spinach salad.*

*Makes 4 servings*

---

2 large red onions, cut into thick rounds
About 2 tablespoons olive oil
Salt

8 cooked smoked sausages, such as kielbasa, duck, Cajun, Polish garlic, or turkey

---

**1.** Brush the onion rounds with the olive oil. Heat a grill pan over medium heat until hot enough to make a few drops of water sizzle. Place the onions on the hot pan and season lightly with salt. Cover loosely with a sheet of aluminum foil and cook until brown grill marks appear on the bottom, 3 to 4 minutes. Using a wide spatula, carefully turn the onion rounds over and cook the second side, loosely covered with the foil, until brown and crisp-tender, about 3 minutes. Transfer the onions to a plate.

**2.** Prick the sausages in several places with a knife or fork and put them on the same grill pan. Cook, turning 2 or 3 times, until brown grill marks appear and the sausages are sizzling hot all the way through, about 10 minutes total. Serve hot.

# Marinated Lamb Loin Chops

*Small lamb loin chops cook quickly on the grill pan. Since they are so small, plan 2 or 3 chops for each serving. Grill them in batches, if your grill pan won't accommodate all the chops at once.*

*Makes 4 servings*

---

8 small loin lamb chops, cut 1 inch thick
¼ cup balsamic vinegar
2 tablespoons olive oil
1 teaspoon fresh lemon juice

1 small garlic clove, crushed through a press
½ teaspoon salt
¼ teaspoon freshly ground pepper

---

**1.** Trim the lamb chops of all excess fat. In a small bowl, whisk together the vinegar, olive oil, lemon juice, garlic, salt, and pepper. Pour into a pie plate. Add the lamb chops and turn to coat. Let marinate at room temperature 30 to 60 minutes.

**2.** Heat a grill pan over medium heat until hot enough to make a few drops of water sizzle. Put the lamb chops on the hot pan and cook until brown and marked from the grill on the bottom, 4 to 5 minutes. Brush with the marinade, turn over, and cook the second side for 3 to 4 minutes for medium-rare or to the desired degree of doneness.

# Lamb Steaks with Sweet Peppers and Onions

*Here's a quick, tasty supper for busy days. Lamb steaks cut from the leg are lean and easy to cook on the grill pan. If lamb steaks are not available in your market's meat case, ask the butcher to cut some for you from the leg. This dish has lots of color, flavor, and texture. To complete the plate, add rice or couscous, and pass a bowl of mango chutney.*

*Makes 4 servings*

---

4 lamb steaks (about 6 ounces each),
   cut from the leg, about ½ inch thick
2 garlic cloves, finely chopped
2 tablespoons olive oil
½ teaspoon salt
⅛ teaspoon freshly ground pepper

1 medium onion, sliced
1 small green bell pepper, cut crosswise
   into rings and seeded
1 small red bell pepper, cut crosswise
   into rings and seeded

---

**1.** Trim all excess fat from the lamb. Rub the steaks all over with the garlic and 1 tablespoon of the olive oil. Season with the salt and pepper.

**2.** In a medium bowl, toss the onion and bell peppers with the remaining olive oil. Heat a grill pan over medium heat until hot enough to make a few drops of water sizzle. Put the onions and peppers on the hot pan and cook, turning often with tongs, until the vegetables are crisp-tender, 3 to 5 minutes. Remove to a bowl.

**3.** Lay the lamb steaks on the hot pan and cook until brown grill marks appear on the bottom, 4 to 5 minutes. Turn the steaks over, and cook until brown on the second side and still pink inside, 3 to 4 minutes. Serve the steaks with the peppers and onions scattered on top.

# Lamb Strips with Lentils

*Nutritious lentils stewed with winter vegetables and strips of lean grilled lamb make a hearty cold weather meal.*

*Makes 4 servings*

---

1½ cups brown or green lentils, picked over

2 bay leaves

1 teaspoon dried oregano

3 tablespoons olive oil

½ medium onion, finely chopped

2 large garlic cloves, finely chopped

2 medium carrots, peeled and finely diced

1 medium turnip, peeled and finely diced

½ medium green bell pepper, finely diced

½ cup chicken broth

⅛ teaspoon crushed hot red pepper

2 tablespoons chopped parsley

Salt and freshly ground pepper

1½ pounds lean lamb steaks, cut from the leg, about ½ inch thick

---

**1.** Rinse the lentils in a wire strainer and put them into a large saucepan. Add the bay leaves and oregano. Cover with water by 2 inches. Bring to a boil over high heat. Reduce the heat to medium-low and simmer the lentils, uncovered, until tender, 25 to 30 minutes. Drain the lentils but do not rinse. Remove and discard the bay leaves. Return the lentils to the pan and reserve off heat.

**2.** In a medium skillet, heat 1½ tablespoons of the olive oil over medium heat. Add the onion and garlic and cook, stirring, until the onion softens, 3 to 4 minutes. Add the carrots, turnip, bell pepper, chicken broth, and hot pepper. Bring to a boil, reduce the heat to medium-low, cover, and cook until the carrots and turnip are barely tender,

4 to 5 minutes. Add the cooked vegetables and the parsley to the pan with the lentils. Stir gently to combine. Season with salt and pepper to taste.

**3.** Trim all excess fat from the lamb steaks. Brush the meat with the remaining 1½ tablespoons olive oil and season lightly with salt and pepper. Heat a grill pan over medium heat until hot enough to make a few drops of water sizzle. Put the lamb steaks on the hot pan and cook until brown grill marks appear on the bottom, 4 to 5 minutes. Turn the steaks over and cook the second side until brown on the bottom and slightly pink inside, 3 to 4 minutes.

**4.** Transfer the meat to a cutting board and let stand for a few minutes, then cut into strips about ⅜ inch wide. To serve, divide the lentils equally among 4 serving plates. Top with the grilled lamb strips.

# Lamb Kebabs with Zucchini

*For these kebabs, choose tender meat from the leg. This succulent grilled lamb goes very well with rice pilaf and cherry tomatoes for color.*

*Makes 4 servings*

---

½ cup dry red wine

2 tablespoons olive oil

1 teaspoon soy sauce

1 shallot, chopped

1 garlic clove, minced

1½ teaspoons dried oregano

½ teaspoon salt

¼ teaspoon freshly ground pepper

2 pounds lean boneless lamb, cut into 1½-inch cubes

1 medium zucchini, cut into ⅜-inch rounds

2 tablespoons prepared vinaigrette of choice

---

**1.** In a mixing bowl, combine the wine, olive oil, soy sauce, shallot, garlic, oregano, salt, and pepper. Add the lamb cubes and toss to coat. Cover and refrigerate about 8 hours or overnight, tossing 2 or 3 times.

**2.** Remove the lamb from the marinade and pat dry with paper towels. Discard the marinade. Brush the zucchini with the vinaigrette. Thread the meat cubes and zucchini together onto metal skewers.

**3.** Heat a grill pan over medium heat until hot enough to make a few drops of water sizzle. Put the lamb kebabs on the hot pan and cook until nicely browned and marked from the grill on the bottom, 3 to 4 minutes. Turn and cook the second side until the lamb is brown on the outside and still pink in the center and the zucchini is barely tender, 2 to 3 minutes longer. Remove the kebabs to a small platter.

**4.** Pour 2 to 3 tablespoons water onto the hot pan to deglaze it. Pour the meat juices over the kebabs and serve at once.

# Lamb Patties with Tomato-Mint Relish

*A quick fresh relish here perks up simple lamb patties. Serve with orzo or mashed potatoes and steamed asparagus.*

*Makes 4 servings*

---

1½ pounds lean ground lamb
2 tablespoons chopped parsley
1 tablespoon fresh lemon juice
1½ teaspoons Worcestershire sauce
1 large garlic clove, crushed through a
   press
1 teaspoon salt
¼ teaspoon freshly ground pepper

2 large ripe tomatoes, seeded and
   chopped
1 fresh jalapeño pepper, seeded and
   minced
¼ cup finely chopped white onion
¼ cup chopped fresh mint
1 tablespoon vegetable oil
Juice of 1 lime

---

**1.** In a medium bowl, mix together the ground lamb, parsley, lemon juice, Worcestershire, garlic, ½ teaspoon of the salt, and the pepper. Form into 8 small patties about ½ inch thick. Set aside while preparing the tomato-mint relish.

**2.** In another bowl, mix together the tomatoes, jalapeño, onion, mint, oil, lime juice, and remaining ½ teaspoon salt. Set the relish aside at room temperature.

**3.** Heat a grill pan over medium heat until hot enough to make a few drops of water sizzle. Put the lamb patties on the hot pan and cook, turning once or twice, until brown on the outside and slightly pink in the center, 8 to 10 minutes total. Serve the patties hot, with the tomato-mint relish on the side.

## Chapter Five

# Grilling Larger Cuts: Seared and Roasted

Larger cuts of meat, or those that need longer cooking times, are quickly browned on the grill pan, and then put into the oven to roast to the proper doneness. It's a technique used by restaurant chefs everywhere. Now, you, too, can get excellent results using the same method with your grill pan. Most grill pan models can go directly from the stove right into a preheated 350 degree F. oven. The oven temperature should not exceed 350 degrees F., unless the instructions for your particular grill pan state that a higher temperature is all right. If a recipe calls for an oven temperature higher than 350 degrees F., or the dish is oven-braised in a sauce, simply transfer the food to an ovenproof baking pan for the final roasting or braising.

The grill pan may not be used often for cooking larger cuts of meat or poultry, but whenever quick searing is desired to give food a browner exterior, you will find the grill pan very useful. When a cut of meat is more than 2 inches thick, this method of a stove-top start combined with an oven finish will work very well. Among the recipes in this chapter are Grilled Game Hens with Garlic, Oregano, and Chili Rub, Butterflied Leg of Lamb, Pork Roast with Szechuan Chile Sauce, and Chicken Legs in Spicy Barbecue Sauce.

# Chicken Thighs with Sun-Dried Tomatoes

*Chicken thighs get a start on the grill pan, and then finish to fork tenderness in the oven.*

*Makes 4 servings*

---

2 tablespoons olive oil
1 medium onion, quartered and thinly sliced
2 garlic cloves, thinly sliced
⅓ cup white wine or dry vermouth
½ cup oil-packed sun-dried tomatoes, thinly sliced

1 teaspoon Worcestershire sauce
½ teaspoon dried marjoram
¼ teaspoon dried thyme
2 tablespoons chopped parsley
8 skinless chicken thighs, on the bone
Salt and freshly ground pepper

---

**1.** In a medium skillet, heat 1 tablespoon of the oil over medium heat. Add the onion and garlic. Cook, stirring, until the onion and garlic begin to brown, about 3 minutes. Add the wine, tomatoes, Worcestershire, marjoram, and thyme. Bring to a boil, and cook 1 minute. Stir in the parsley. Set aside off the heat.

**2.** Preheat the oven to 350 degrees F. Trim the chicken thighs of all visible fat. Brush the thighs with the remaining 1 tablespoon of oil, and season with salt and pepper. Heat a grill pan over medium heat until hot enough to make a few drops of water sizzle. Put the thighs on the heated pan, skin sides down, and cook in batches of 4 at a time, until brown grill marks appear, 5 to 6 minutes. Turn the thighs, and cook the second side for 3 minutes.

**3.** Transfer the thighs to an ovenproof baking dish. Spoon the sauce over the thighs, cover, and put in the preheated oven. Cook the thighs for 45 to 50 minutes, or until very tender.

# Chicken Breasts Stuffed with Feta Cheese, Olives, and Sun-Dried Tomatoes

*This excellent recipe for stuffed chicken breasts starts the chicken on the stove-top in the grill pan. Then the pan and the chicken go directly into the oven to thoroughly cook the stuffing. To hold the stuffing, you want the skin on, but for quicker cooking, I've eliminated the bone. You may have to ask your butcher to bone the chicken breasts for you, leaving the skin on. Buttered orzo and steamed spinach would make fine accompaniments to this savory dish.*

*Makes 4 servings*

---

4 boneless chicken breast halves, skin left on

2 teaspoons olive oil

½ cup mild feta cheese, crumbled

¼ cup finely chopped toasted slivered almonds

2 tablespoons pitted and chopped kalamata olives

2 tablespoons finely chopped onion

2 tablespoons chopped oil-packed sun-dried tomatoes

½ teaspoon dried marjoram

½ teaspoon salt

⅛ teaspoon freshly ground pepper

---

**1.** Trim the chicken breasts of excess skin and visible fat. With a sharp knife, slit each breast lengthwise, making a pocket as wide as possible without cutting through the edges on three sides. Rub the olive oil over the outside of the breasts.

**2.** Preheat the oven to 350 degrees F. In a medium bowl, mix together the feta cheese, almonds, olives, onion, tomatoes, and marjoram. Fill each chicken breast pocket equally with the mixture. Season the skin sides of the breasts with the salt and pepper.

**3.** Heat a grill pan over medium heat until hot enough to make a few drops of water sizzle. Put the stuffed breasts on the hot pan, skin sides down, and cook until brown grill marks appear on the bottom, 3 to 4 minutes. Turn the breasts over and cook the second side for 2 minutes.

**4.** Transfer the grill pan with the chicken to the preheated oven. Roast 20 to 25 minutes, or until the meat is white throughout but still juicy. Serve hot.

# Chicken Legs in Spicy Barbecue Sauce

*Pick up as much smoke as possible from the grill, then finish off these generous bone-in pieces in the oven. Serve with potato salad, corn on the cob, and a bright tomato salad.*

*Makes 4 servings*

---

1 teaspoon vegetable oil
1 medium shallot, minced
½ teaspoon dried oregano
½ cup ketchup
1 tablespoon Dijon mustard
1 tablespoon honey
1 tablespoon frozen orange juice concentrate (undiluted)

2 teaspoons Worcestershire sauce
1 teaspoon finely chopped parsley
⅛ teaspoon crushed hot red pepper
4 chicken legs (6 to 8 ounces each)
Salt

---

**1.** In a small saucepan, heat the oil over medium heat. Add the shallot and oregano and cook, stirring, until the shallot just begins to color, 2 to 3 minutes. Add the ketchup, mustard, honey, orange juice concentrate, Worcestershire, parsley, and hot pepper. Bring to a boil, stirring, and cook about 30 seconds. Set the barbecue sauce aside.

**2.** Preheat the oven to 350 degrees F. Coat a grill pan with nonstick cooking spray, then heat over medium heat until hot enough to make a few drops of water sizzle. Season the chicken lightly with salt and put on the hot pan, skin sides down. Cook until golden brown on the bottom, 5 to 6 minutes. Turn the chicken pieces over and cook the second side for 4 minutes.

**3.** Transfer the chicken legs, skin sides up, to a rack on a foil-lined baking sheet and brush the tops with a thin coat of the barbecue sauce. Place on the middle shelf of the preheated oven and bake, uncovered, for 20 minutes.

**4.** Turn the legs over and brush with barbecue sauce. Bake the chicken legs 20 minutes longer. Turn the legs over again and brush with the remaining sauce. Cook until the legs are very tender, with no trace of pink near the bone, about 15 minutes. Serve the chicken hot or warm.

# Chicken Breasts with Tomato-Wine Sauce

*Many cooks agree that meat cooked on the bone has more flavor, and the skin helps to keep the chicken from drying out. This recipe calls for chicken breasts on the bone with the skin left on. The chicken is quickly browned on the grill pan, and then finished in the oven. Oven-roasted potatoes make an appealing accompaniment.*

*Makes 4 servings*

3 tablespoons olive oil
1 medium onion, chopped
3 garlic cloves, finely chopped
1 teaspoon dried thyme leaves or 2 teaspoons minced fresh thyme
½ teaspoon dried oregano
½ cup dry red wine, such as Chianti or zinfandel
½ cup chicken broth

1 cup canned diced tomatoes, drained
10 kalamata olives, pitted and sliced
¼ teaspoon crushed hot red pepper
¼ teaspoon Maggi concentrated liquid seasoning
1 tablespoon chopped flat-leaf parsley
Salt and freshly ground pepper
4 chicken breast halves, on the bone with skin

**1.** Preheat the oven to 350 degrees F. In a medium saucepan, heat 2 tablespoons of the olive oil over medium heat. Add the onion, garlic, thyme, and oregano. Cook, stirring frequently, until the onions are lightly browned, 4 to 5 minutes. Add the wine and cook, stirring, until the wine is reduced by half. Add the chicken broth, tomatoes, olives, hot pepper, Maggi seasoning, and parsley. Reduce the heat to low and simmer the sauce, uncovered, for 10 minutes. Season to taste with salt and pepper. Set the sauce aside.

**2.** Heat a grill pan over medium heat until hot enough to make a few drops of water sizzle. Brush the chicken breasts with the remaining 1 tablespoon olive oil and season lightly with salt and pepper. Put the breasts on the heated pan, skin sides down, and cook until brown grill marks appear, 4 to 5 minutes. Turn the chicken over and cook the second side for 3 minutes.

**3.** Transfer the grill pan and the chicken directly to the preheated oven. Roast until the breasts are cooked through, white near the bone but still juicy, 20 to 25 minutes.

**4.** Reheat the sauce. Spoon some of the sauce over each chicken breast. Pass the remainder on the side.

# Game Hens with Thai Red Curry Sauce

*Discover the exotic flavor of Thailand's fiery red curry sauce served on grilled game hens. It's easy with the help of prepared HOT Thai red curry paste. It's essential to serve steamed rice with this dish; try Thai jasmine rice. The curry paste and the rice are available in many supermarkets or at Asian specialty markets.*

*Makes 4 servings*

1½ cups canned unsweetened coconut milk

1 to 2 teaspoons Thai red curry paste (1 teaspoon for moderate heat, 2 for fiery)

1 lemongrass stalk, cut into 2-inch pieces

1½ tablespoons vegetable oil

1½ tablespoons fresh lime juice

2 large garlic cloves, crushed through a press

½ teaspoon salt

2 (1¼-pound) game hens, halved lengthwise, rinsed, and blotted dry

Steamed rice, for serving

1 large mango, cut in ½-inch-thick slices

3 tablespoons coarsely chopped cilantro

**1.** In a heavy medium saucepan, whisk together the coconut milk and curry paste. Add the lemongrass. Bring to a boil over medium heat and continue to boil, stirring frequently, until the sauce is reduced to 1 cup, 10 to 12 minutes. The sauce will coat the back of a wooden spoon. Remove and discard the lemongrass. Set the curry sauce aside.

**2.** Preheat the oven to 375 degrees F. Make a moist paste of the oil, lime juice, garlic, and salt. Rub the paste all over the game hens. Fold the wing tips under the top of the shoulder. Spray a grill pan with nonstick cooking spray, and then heat the grill pan over medium heat until hot enough to make a few drops of water sizzle. Put the hens on the heated pan, skin sides down, and cook until brown grill marks appear on the legs and breasts, 4 to 5 minutes. Turn the hens over, and cook 3 minutes longer.

**3.** Transfer the hens on the grill pan to the preheated oven. Roast 25 to 30 minutes, or until the skin is crisp and brown and the thigh juices run clear when pierced with the tip of a sharp knife.

**4.** To serve, reheat the sauce and pool ¼ cup of the curry sauce on each of 4 serving plates. Place one grilled hen half over the sauce on each plate. Spoon some steamed rice alongside. Arrange the mango slices equally on each plate. Sprinkle one-fourth of the chopped cilantro over each serving.

# Grilled Game Hens with Garlic, Oregano, and Chili Rub

*Cutting the game hens in half before grilling makes them easier to handle and shortens the total cooking time. To achieve the distinctive grill marks and crisp skin, start cooking the hens on the stove-top grill pan, then finish them off in the oven.*

*Makes 2 servings*

---

2 game hens (about 1¼ pounds each)
3 large garlic cloves, crushed through a
  press
1½ teaspoons dried oregano

1½ teaspoons chili powder
1 teaspoon salt
¼ teaspoon freshly ground pepper
2½ tablespoons vegetable oil

---

**1.** Remove the giblets from the cavity and trim the excess fat from the game hens. With a large knife, game shears, or a cleaver, cut the birds in half lengthwise along the edge of the back bone. Remove the back bone and discard. Rinse the birds and blot with paper towels. Fold the wing tips under the top of the shoulders.

**2.** In a small bowl, combine the garlic, oregano, chili powder, salt, pepper, and vegetable oil to make a pastelike mixture. Rub the seasoning mixture all over the game hem halves.

**3.** Preheat the oven to 375 degrees F. Spray a grill pan with nonstick cooking spray, then heat the pan over medium heat until hot enough to make a few drops of water sizzle. Put the hens, skin sides down, on the hot pan and cook until brown grill marks appear on the bottom, 5 to 6 minutes. Turn the hens over and cook 3 minutes.

**4.** Transfer the hens on the grill pan to the preheated oven. Roast for 20 to 25 minutes, or until the skins are crisp and brown and the thigh juices run clear when pierced with the tip of a sharp knife.

# Grilled and Roasted Beef Tenderloin

*Beef tenderloin is outstanding for a special menu, and this method of prepara-*
*tion is easy and reliable. For this recipe, you will need a baking pan with a*
*rack as well as the stove-top grill pan.*

*Makes 8 to 10 servings*

---

| | |
|---|---|
| 1 (5-pound) beef tenderloin, trimmed of all fat and silver membrane | ½ teaspoon salt |
| 3 garlic cloves, crushed | ½ teaspoon freshly ground pepper |
| | 2 tablespoons olive oil |

---

**1.** Put the tenderloin on a large platter. In a small bowl, make a paste of the garlic, salt, pepper, and olive oil. Rub the mixture all over the meat. Let the meat stand for about 30 minutes.

**2.** Have a baking pan with a rack ready. Preheat the oven to 425 degrees F. Heat a grill pan over medium heat until hot enough to make a few drops of water sizzle. Put the tenderloin on the heated pan, and cook, turning several times, until marked with brown from the grill on all sides.

**3.** Transfer the meat to the rack in the baking pan, and place in the middle of the preheated oven. Cook, uncovered, 40 to 50 minutes, or until a meat thermometer registers 150 degrees F. for medium-rare. Remove the meat from the oven and let rest 8 to 10 minutes before slicing.

# Braised Boneless Beef Short Ribs with Vegetable Confetti

*These boneless beef short ribs with a rich brown Asian-flavored sauce are terrific. Brown the beef on the grill pan, and finish in the oven to intensify the flavor and tenderize the meat. For an up-to-date presentation, surround the meat with colorful bits of sautéed vegetables.*

*Makes 4 servings*

---

2 garlic cloves, chopped
2 tablespoons rice vinegar
2 tablespoons soy sauce
2 teaspoons ketchup
2 teaspoons sugar
1 teaspoon minced fresh ginger
1 teaspoon Asian sesame oil
1 scallion, chopped
1 pound boneless beef short ribs, trimmed of any fat
1 tablespoon vegetable oil
1 tablespoon olive oil

1 medium green zucchini, cut into ¼-inch dice
1 medium yellow zucchini, cut into ¼-inch dice
1 medium carrot, peeled and cut into ¼-inch dice
½ red bell pepper, cut into ¼-inch dice
3 tablespoons diced red onion
1 teaspoon balsamic vinegar
Salt and freshly ground pepper

---

**1.** Preheat the oven to 350 degrees F. In a medium bowl, mix together the garlic, rice vinegar, soy sauce, ketchup, sugar, ginger, sesame oil, and chopped scallion. Set aside.

**2.** Brush the beef with the vegetable oil. Heat a grill pan over medium heat until hot enough to make a few drops of water sizzle, then put the short ribs on the heated pan. Cook the meat, turning 3 to 4 times, until brown on all sides, 6 to 8 minutes. Transfer the meat to an ovenproof baking dish. Pour the sauce over the meat, cover, and roast for one hour.

**3.** Meanwhile, in a medium nonstick skillet, heat the olive oil over medium heat. Add the green and yellow zucchini, carrot, bell pepper, and red onion. Cook, stirring, until the vegetables are crisp-tender, about 5 minutes. Stir in the balsamic vinegar. Season to taste with salt and pepper. Set aside.

**4.** After an hour, remove the cover from the meat, and turn the pieces over. Cook the beef, uncovered, for 20 to 25 minutes, or until about 3 tablespoons of sauce remain in the baking dish. To serve, divide the beef equally and place in the centers of 4 serving plates. Spoon the sauce juices over each serving. Reheat the vegetables, and spoon equally around the meat on the plates.

# Pork Roast with Szechuan Chile Sauce

*From stove-top to oven, the grill pan makes roasting this way an easy task. I credit the spicy sauce to my friend, Joyce Jue.*

*Makes 4 servings*

---

2 tablespoons vegetable oil
1 tablespoon minced garlic
1 tablespoon minced fresh ginger
3 tablespoons sugar
2 tablespoons tomato paste
2 to 3 teaspoons Chinese red chile paste, to taste
⅓ cup canned chicken broth

¼ cup dry vermouth or rice wine
1½ tablespoons soy sauce
½ teaspoon cornstarch
3 tablespoons red wine vinegar
1½ teaspoons Asian sesame oil
1 (2-pound) boneless pork loin
½ teaspoon salt
¼ teaspoon freshly ground pepper

---

**1.** In a small saucepan, heat 1 tablespoon of the vegetable oil over medium heat. Add the garlic and ginger. Cook, stirring, until fragrant, 20 to 30 seconds. Add the sugar, tomato paste, and chile paste. Cook, stirring, to a thick and sticky glaze, 3 to 4 minutes. Add the broth and vermouth. Stir together the soy sauce and cornstarch until blended and smooth. Stir into the sauce. Raise the heat to medium-high and bring to a boil, stirring, until slightly thickened, 1 to 2 minutes. Stir in the vinegar and sesame oil. Cook 1 minute. Remove the pan from the heat and strain the sauce to remove the solids. Return the sauce to the saucepan. Cover and reserve.

**2.** Preheat the oven to 375 degrees F. Trim any excess fat from the pork loin. Brush the roast lightly with the remaining 1 tablespoon oil and season with the salt and pepper. Heat a grill pan over medium heat until hot enough to make a few drops of water sizzle. Put the pork on the pan, fat side down, and cook until brown on the bottom, 5 to 6 minutes. Turn the roast over and transfer the grill pan to the preheated oven.

**3.** Roast until an instant-read thermometer registers 160 degrees F. and the meat is no longer pink in the center, 35 to 40 minutes. Remove the roast to a cutting board and let stand about 5 minutes. Meanwhile, reheat the sauce over low heat. Carve the roast and pass the sauce on the side.

# Pork Tenderloin with Onion
# and Mustard Cream Sauce

*Pork tenderloin is one of the most dependable cuts of meat to prepare and serve. I like to sear the meat quickly on the grill pan and then let it finish cooking in the oven while I tend to the rest of the meal. The creamy sauce tastes rich and luxurious with the lean pork.*

*Makes 4 servings*

---

2 tablespoons unsalted butter
1 medium onion, finely chopped
¼ cup dry vermouth
½ cup chicken broth
½ cup Dijon mustard
¾ cup heavy cream

Salt and freshly ground pepper
3 whole pork tenderloins (about
   1 pound each)
2 teaspoons olive oil
Chopped parsley

---

**1.** In a medium saucepan, melt the butter over medium-low heat. Add the onion, cover, and cook, stirring frequently, until the onion is light brown, 4 to 5 minutes. Add the vermouth, broth, and mustard. Bring to a boil, and cook, uncovered, stirring, for 1 minute. Pour in the cream and continue cooking, stirring frequently, until the sauce reduces and thickens enough to coat the back of a wooden spoon, about 5 minutes. Season with salt and pepper to taste. Remove the sauce from the heat and set aside.

**2.** Preheat the oven to 375 degrees F. Trim the tenderloins of all silvery membrane. Brush the meat with the olive oil and season lightly with salt and pepper. Heat a grill pan over medium heat until hot enough to make a few drops of water sizzle. Put the tenderloins on the hot pan and cook until brown grill marks appear, 4 to 5 minutes. Turn the meat over and brown the second side, about 3 minutes.

**3.** Transfer the grill pan and the tenderloins to the preheated oven. Roast for 25 minutes, or until an instant-read thermometer registers 160 degrees F.

**4.** Remove the tenderloins from the oven and let stand for about 5 minutes before slicing. Meanwhile, reheat the sauce. Slice the meat and arrange it on a platter or individual plates. Ladle the sauce over the pork, garnish with a dusting of chopped parsley, and serve.

# Pork Tenderloin with Red Pepper Relish

*First make the easy sauce for the delicious pork tenderloins. Use the grill pan to brand the meat with grill marks. Then let the oven finish the cooking.*

*Makes 4 to 6 servings*

½ (7-ounce) jar roasted red peppers, drained and chopped

2 tablespoons plus 2 teaspoons olive oil

1 tablespoon chopped parsley

1 teaspoon soy sauce

1 teaspoon red wine vinegar

1 teaspoon drained capers

⅛ teaspoon Tabasco or other hot sauce

2 whole pork tenderloins (12 to 16 ounces each)

2 garlic cloves, crushed through a press

½ teaspoon dried oregano

½ teaspoon salt

¼ teaspoon freshly ground pepper

**1.** In a medium bowl, combine the roasted peppers, 2 tablespoons of the olive oil, the parsley, soy sauce, vinegar, capers, and Tabasco. Let the red pepper relish stand at room temperature for 1 to 4 hours or cover and refrigerate for up to 5 days.

**2.** Preheat the oven to 375 degrees F. Trim the tenderloins of all silvery membrane. Make a paste of the remaining 2 teaspoons of olive oil, the garlic, oregano, salt, and pepper. Rub the seasoning paste all over the pork.

**3.** Heat a grill pan over medium heat until hot enough to make a few drops of water sizzle. Add the tenderloins and cook, turning, until browned all over, 5 to 7 minutes.

**4.** Transfer the grill pan with the tenderloins to the preheated oven. Roast for 25 minutes, or until an instant-read thermometer registers 160 degrees F. Let the meat rest 3 to 5 minutes before slicing. Spoon the red pepper relish over each serving.

# Roasted Pork Tenderloin with Spiced Chili Rub

*Dry seasoning rubs are a popular way to add lots of flavor to grilled and roasted meats. The proportions I give below make more chili rub than you'll need for this one recipe. The remainder can be stored in a sealed plastic bag, or covered container, and frozen for up to three months.*

*Makes 4 to 6 servings*

---

2 pork tenderloins (about 12 ounces each)
1 tablespoon vegetable oil

2 to 3 tablespoons spiced chili rub (recipe follows)

---

**1.** Remove the silvery membrane from the pork. Brush the oil over the tenderloins. Spoon about 2 tablespoons of the chili rub onto a plate and roll the tenderloins in the seasonings to coat all over. Let the pork tenderloins stand at room temperature for about 20 minutes.

**2.** Preheat the oven to 450 degrees F. Heat a grill pan over medium heat until hot enough to make a few drops of water sizzle. Put the tenderloins on the hot pan and cook, turning, until browned, 5 to 7 minutes.

**3.** Transfer the meat to a baking sheet and roast in the preheated oven for about 15 minutes, or until white throughout but still juicy. Let stand for a few minutes before slicing.

# Spiced Chili Rub

*Store any extra spice rub in a self-sealing plastic bag in the freezer.*

*Makes about ½ cup*

---

3 tablespoons cumin seeds
1 tablespoon coriander seeds
½ teaspoon aniseeds
1½ tablespoons dried oregano, preferably
Mexican

¼ cup pure New Mexico chili powder
2 tablespoons dark brown sugar
1 teaspoon salt

---

**1.** In a dry medium skillet, preferably nonstick, toast the cumin, coriander, aniseeds, and oregano over medium heat, stirring, until fragrant, 2 to 3 minutes. Remove to a plate or bowl and let cool for about 5 minutes.

**2.** Grind the toasted ingredients to a powder in a spice grinder or coffee mill. Place in a bowl. Add the chili powder, brown sugar, and salt. Mix very well. Freeze any leftover rub in a small plastic freezer bag or covered container for up to 3 months.

# Lamb with Spanish Sofrito

*Sofrito consists of aromatic vegetables, and sometimes bits of ham, cooked together slowly. Here the lamb is browned on the grill pan and then placed atop the sofrito to finish cooking. An earthenware casserole is ideal for the oven portion of this recipe.*

*Makes 4 servings*

---

2 tablespoons plus 2 teaspoons olive oil

1 large onion, finely chopped

3 garlic cloves, finely chopped

1 medium green bell pepper, seeded and finely chopped

4 ripe tomatoes, peeled and chopped, or 1½ cups chopped canned tomatoes

2 tablespoons dry sherry or vermouth

2 tablespoons finely chopped parsley

½ cup chopped ham

Salt and freshly ground pepper

4 round-bone lamb steaks cut from the leg (7 to 8 ounces each), about ½ inch thick, trimmed of excess fat

---

**1.** In a large skillet, heat 2 tablespoons of oil over medium heat. Add the onion, garlic, and bell pepper. Cook, stirring, until the vegetables soften, 4 to 5 minutes. Add the tomatoes, sherry, parsley, and ham. Cook, stirring frequently, until the juices are reduced and the mixture thickens, about 4 minutes. Season to taste with salt and pepper. Spread the sofrito evenly in an 8-by-11-inch baking dish and set aside.

**2.** Preheat the oven to 350 degrees F. Brush the remaining 2 teaspoons of oil on the lamb steaks. Season with salt and pepper. Heat a grill pan over medium heat until hot enough to make a few drops of water sizzle. Put the lamb on the heated pan, and cook until brown grill marks appear, 4 to 5 minutes. Turn the lamb, and cook the second side for 3 minutes. Put the lamb steaks on top of the sofrito in the casserole.

**3.** Cover with foil and place in the preheated oven. Bake for 30 to 35 minutes, or until the sauce is bubbling and the lamb is tender. Serve from the casserole.

# Butterflied Leg of Lamb

*A leg of lamb suits just about any special occasion. It cooks faster and is easier to carve when it's boneless. Ask your butcher to do the boning. The lamb will be easier to handle on the grill pan if the meat is separated into 2 or 3 sections along the natural muscle lines. The boned meat may not be of uniform thickness, so be sure to use an instant-read thermometer to test for doneness in the thickest part. Some people like rare slices of lamb and others prefer medium or well-done, so I find it best to offer some of each.*

*Makes 6 servings*

---

1 (4½- to 5-pound) leg of lamb, boned and butterflied (2 to 2½ pounds of boned meat)
¼ cup olive oil
3 large garlic cloves, crushed through a press

2 teaspoons chopped fresh rosemary or 1 teaspoon dried, crumbled
1 tablespoon red wine vinegar
1 teaspoon soy sauce
1 teaspoon sea salt or coarse kosher salt
½ teaspoon freshly ground pepper

---

**1.** Trim the excess fat and tendons from the lamb and separate the meat into large pieces where it divides naturally. Put the lamb in a glass baking dish that just holds the pieces in a single layer.

**2.** In a small bowl, combine the olive oil, garlic, rosemary, vinegar, soy sauce, salt, and pepper. Pour the marinade over the lamb and turn the meat several times to coat all over. Cover and refrigerate for at least 6 hours or overnight. Let the meat return to room temperature before cooking.

**3.** Preheat the oven to 350 degrees F. Heat a grill pan over medium heat until hot enough to make a few drops of water sizzle. Lay the lamb on the hot pan and cook, turning 2 or 3 times, until the lamb is brown on both sides, 8 to 10 minutes total.

**4.** Transfer the lamb on the grill pan to the preheated oven. Roast for 20 to 25 minutes, or until an instant-read thermometer registers 130 to 135 degrees F. for medium-rare when inserted in the thickest part of the meat, or cook to the desired degree of doneness. Put the lamb on a cutting board and let stand for 8 to 10 minutes. Carve into slices, collecting any juices to spoon over the meat.

## Chapter Six
# Grilled Vegetables

What a revelation it is to learn how successfully vegetables cook on the grill pan and how fantastic they taste. Most vegetables take well to grilling, and they cook in less time than one might imagine. Since grilled vegetables are often served at room temperature, they can be cooked ahead. That leaves the grill pan ready for cooking another part of the meal.

Shop for fresh seasonal vegetables, and select the best available to cook on the grill pan. It's best to choose smaller vegetables that are fresh and young. Larger vegetables must be cut into uniformly sized pieces for quicker cooking and better flavor because more surfaces will sear by being in contact with the grill. To obtain a smoky flavor, to prevent sticking, and to retain moisture, the vegetables are first brushed or tossed lightly with oil. To cook vegetables faster and to keep them moist, some of the recipes in this book suggest covering the vegetables with a tent of aluminum foil. A large dome-shaped lid will work, too.

These recipes will add beautiful color, good texture, and great flavor to your menus. For example, in spring, try Snappy Sugar Snap Peas or Asparagus with Mustard Butter; in summer, Grilled Corn on the Cob or Baby Sunburst Squash with Cheese Topping. In the fall, try Garlic Eggplant Steaks or Grilled Red Bell Peppers, Onions, and Portobello Mushrooms. Winter fare could be Crunchy Grilled Cabbage Wedges or Cauliflower with Asiago Cream Sauce and Ham.

# Asparagus with Mustard Butter

*Choose bright green asparagus that's firm and straight. To be sure the stalks cook through evenly, it's best to blanch them in boiling water for a minute or two before cooking on the grill pan. This can be served as a side dish or as a first course.*

*Makes 4 servings*

---

3 tablespoons butter, at room
   temperature
1 tablespoon Dijon mustard
1 tablespoon fresh lemon juice
¼ teaspoon freshly ground pepper

1 pound medium asparagus, tough
   stems removed
1 tablespoon olive oil
½ teaspoon salt

---

**1.** In a small bowl, mix together the butter, mustard, lemon juice, and pepper. Set the mustard butter aside.

**2.** In a large pot of boiling water, cook the asparagus for 2 minutes. Drain immediately and put the spears on a platter. Blot with paper towels to remove as much moisture as possible. Drizzle the oil over the asparagus and roll the spears around to coat them with the oil. Sprinkle with the salt.

**3.** Heat a grill pan over medium heat until hot enough to make a few drops of water sizzle. Put the asparagus on the hot pan and cook until grill marks appear on the bottom, 3 to 4 minutes. Turn the spears over and cook 2 minutes longer for crisp-tender spears. Serve immediately with the mustard butter.

# Belgian Endive with Lemon Butter

*Belgian endive has a slightly bitter taste, which many people enjoy. Cooking mellows that bitterness, and grilling caramelizes the vegetable, bringing out its natural sweetness. When shopping for Belgian endive, look for the whitest heads, ones that feel heavy, with tightly closed leaves and very little green.*

*Makes 4 servings*

---

| | |
|---|---|
| 8 heads of Belgian endive | 2 tablespoons melted butter |
| 1½ tablespoons olive oil | 1 tablespoon fresh lemon juice |
| Salt | Freshly ground pepper |

---

**1.** Trim a thin slice off the stem end of each endive and pull off and discard any discolored outer leaves. Cut the endive in half lengthwise. Brush generously with the olive oil and season lightly with salt.

**2.** Heat a grill pan over medium heat until hot enough to make a few drops of water sizzle. Lay the endive, cut sides down, on the hot pan and cover loosely with a sheet of aluminum foil. Cook the endives until brown marks appear on the bottom, 4 to 5 minutes. Turn the endives over, reduce the heat to low, and cook the endives, still covered with foil, until they appear wilted and limp, 4 to 5 minutes longer.

**3.** Transfer the endives to a serving plate. Drizzle the melted butter and lemon juice over them. Season with a grinding of fresh pepper. Serve hot or at room temperature.

# Crunchy Grilled Cabbage Wedges

*Smoky-tasting, crunchy wedges of cabbage make an excellent side vegetable with grilled sausages, pork, or steak. The grilled cabbage can also be chopped and made into a uniquely flavored coleslaw. If you prefer softer cabbage, cook it a few minutes longer than the recipe suggests.*

*Makes 4 servings*

---

1 small green cabbage (about ¾ pound)       1 teaspoon coarse kosher salt
2 tablespoons olive oil                                     Freshly ground pepper

---

**1.** Remove the tough outer layer of leaves from the cabbage. Cut the cabbage into 8 equal wedges, leaving the center core attached to hold the leaves together. Pour the oil onto a plate. Turn the cabbage wedges in the oil, 1 at a time, to coat both sides. Season the wedges with the salt.

**2.** Heat a grill pan over medium heat until hot enough to make a few drops of water sizzle. In batches without crowding, lay the cabbage wedges on the hot pan, cover with a sheet of aluminum foil, and cook, turning and moving the wedges around for even cooking, until they are brown with grill marks on both sides and crisp-tender, 10 to 12 minutes. Season with pepper to taste before serving.

# Cauliflower with Asiago Cream Sauce and Ham

*What a tasty surprise it is to learn how well the grill pan cooks cauliflower. The crisp-tender, brown-flecked pieces have a lightly charred flavor. To dress the cauliflower up still further, a creamy Asiago cheese sauce is spooned over it and strips of pan-grilled ham are scattered on top. Serve this as a special side dish with roast chicken or pork, or match it up with pasta.*

*Makes 4 servings*

---

1½ tablespoons butter
1½ tablespoons flour
½ cup milk (I use low-fat here)
½ cup chicken broth
⅓ cup shredded Asiago cheese
Dash of cayenne

1 head of cauliflower (1½ pounds),
  trimmed and separated into florets
1 tablespoon olive oil
Salt and freshly ground pepper
1 slice of fully cooked ham (8 to
  10 ounces), ¼ inch thick

---

**1.** In a small saucepan, melt the butter over medium heat. Add the flour and cook, whisking, for 1 to 2 minutes. Pour in the milk and broth and bring to a boil, whisking, until thick and smooth. Reduce the heat to low. Stir in the cheese and cayenne. Cook, stirring, until the cheese is melted, 1 to 2 minutes. Cover the pan, remove from the heat, and set aside.

**2.** Cut the large pieces of cauliflower in half and leave the small florets whole. Toss the cauliflower with the olive oil to coat lightly.

**3.** Heat a grill pan over medium heat until hot enough to make a few drops of water sizzle. Put the cauliflower on the hot pan, pushing the pieces close together. Season lightly with salt and pepper. Cover with a sheet of aluminum foil and cook until the pieces are flecked with brown on the bottom, 4 to 5 minutes. Using tongs, turn the pieces over, reduce the heat to medium-low, cover with the foil, and cook 3 minutes longer. Remove the cauliflower to a shallow serving bowl and cover with foil to keep warm.

**4.** Put the ham slice on the hot grill pan. Cook until brown grill marks appear on the bottom, 3 to 4 minutes. Turn the ham over and cook 3 minutes longer. Transfer the ham to a cutting board and slice into thin strips.

**5.** Reheat the cheese sauce, if necessary, and spoon over the cauliflower. Scatter the ham strips over the top. Serve while hot.

# Pan-Roasted Carrots with Cumin

*You can achieve a wonderful roasted flavor in just minutes by cooking carrots on the grill pan. Grilled carrots look pretty sliced on the bias into oblong circles; to get the nicest oblongs, choose the largest carrots you can find. As with other firm vegetables, carrots must be blanched in boiling water to tenderize them before grilling.*

*Makes 4 servings*

---

3 large carrots, peeled and cut crosswise at a sharp angle into oval slices about ¼ inch thick

1 tablespoon vegetable oil
½ teaspoon salt
¼ teaspoon ground cumin

---

**1.** In a medium saucepan, bring 3 cups water to a boil. Add the carrots. When the water returns to a boil, cook them for 1 minute. Drain the carrots and return them to the pan. Add the oil, salt, and cumin. Toss to coat the slices with the seasonings.
**2.** Heat a grill pan over medium heat until hot enough to make a few drops of water sizzle. Lay the carrots on the hot pan in a single layer and cover loosely with a sheet of aluminum foil. Cook the carrots until brown grill marks appear on the bottom, 3 to 4 minutes. Turn the carrots over, cover again with the foil, and cook the second side for 3 minutes.
**3.** Arrange the grilled carrot slices, in an overlapping pattern, on a serving plate. Serve warm.

# Grilled Corn on the Cob

*Corn on the cob is surely one of summer's finest eating treats. At our house, we think the best way to savor its goodness is to enjoy it as a separate course. We also love the slightly smoky, nutty taste of sweet corn cooked on the grill pan. Young corn with small juicy kernels can go directly on the heated pan. Mature corn with larger kernels, or corn that is not extremely fresh, will grill better if blanched for a minute in boiling water first. Either way, cover the ears with foil while they grill to trap the heat.*

*Makes 4 servings*

---

4 ears of fresh corn

2 tablespoons corn oil

Butter, salt, and freshly ground pepper

---

**1.** Husk the corn and brush it with the oil. (If the corn is mature, cook it for 1 minute in a large pot of boiling water first, then brush it with the oil.)

**2.** Heat a grill pan over medium heat until hot enough to make a few drops of water sizzle. Lay the corn on the hot pan, cover loosely with aluminum foil, and cook, turning frequently, until most of the kernels are flecked with brown, 8 to 10 minutes. Serve the hot corn with butter, salt, pepper, and plenty of napkins.

# Eggplant Boats Stuffed with Fresh Tomatoes

*Small Asian eggplants develop a pleasantly smoky outdoor flavor when cooked indoors on the grill pan. These tender eggplant shells with a slightly spicy, herbed tomato filling make a striking side dish.*

*Makes 4 servings*

---

4 slender Asian eggplants (about
   4 ounces each), halved lengthwise
¼ cup olive oil
1 teaspoon salt
¼ teaspoon freshly ground pepper
1 small onion, finely chopped

2 garlic cloves, finely chopped
½ teaspoon dried oregano
¼ teaspoon dried thyme
⅛ teaspoon crushed hot red pepper
4 or 5 plum tomatoes, peeled and diced
1 tablespoon chopped parsley

---

**1.** With a melon-baller, scoop out some of the eggplant pulp, leaving a ⅜-inch-thick shell. Chop the pulp and set aside. Brush the eggplant shells with 2 tablespoons of the olive oil. Season with half the salt and black pepper.

**2.** Heat a grill pan over medium heat until hot enough to make a few drops of water sizzle. Lay the eggplant, cut sides down, on the hot pan. Tent with a sheet of aluminum foil and cook until the eggplant is marked with brown from the grill, 3 to 4 minutes. Turn the shells over and cover again with the foil. Cook until the shells are tender but still hold their shape, 4 to 5 minutes. Remove the eggplant "boats" to a plate.

**3.** In a medium skillet, heat the remaining 2 tablespoons olive oil over medium-high heat. Add the onion, garlic, oregano, thyme, hot pepper, and reserved eggplant pulp. Season with the remaining salt and black pepper. Cook, stirring, until the onion is softened, about 3 minutes. Add the tomatoes, and cook, stirring frequently, until the mixture thickens, 3 to 4 minutes. Stir in the parsley. Spoon the tomato filling into the grilled eggplant boats. Serve warm or at room temperature.

---

# Garlic Eggplant Steaks

*Sliced eggplant does very well on the grill, though you may have to cook it in batches. I turn this into an easy vegetarian main course by topping it with pasta sauce, which I buy if I am in a hurry, and good Parmesan cheese.*

*Makes 4 servings*

---

1 large purple eggplant (about 1½ pounds), peeled and cut into ½-inch-thick rounds.

3 garlic cloves, finely chopped

3 tablespoons extra-virgin olive oil

½ teaspoon salt

⅛ teaspoon freshly ground pepper

Pasta sauce, homemade or purchased, heated

Freshly grated Parmesan cheese

---

**1.** Rub the eggplant rounds with garlic and brush the tops generously with the olive oil. Season the rounds with the salt and pepper. Heat a grill pan over medium heat until hot enough to make a few drops of water sizzle. Put the eggplant rounds, oiled sides down, on the hot pan and brush the tops with olive oil. Cook until brown grill marks appear on the bottom, 2 to 3 minutes. Without turning, rotate the slices 90 degrees and cook for another 1 to 2 minutes to make cross-hatched marks. Turn the rounds over and grill the second side until the eggplant is soft, another 2 to 3 minutes.

**2.** Serve the eggplant "steaks" topped with heated pasta sauce and sprinkled liberally with Parmesan cheese.

# Spicy Grilled Okra

*Fresh young okra, only about 2 inches long, are tender and mild. If you cook them whole for a short time, they will remain slightly crisp and will not produce any of the slimy quality so often associated with okra. This makes an interesting and tasty accent vegetable with chicken, pork, or fish.*

*Makes 4 servings*

---

¾ pound fresh small okra (about 2 inches long)

3 tablespoons olive oil

½ teaspoon salt

⅛ teaspoon freshly ground pepper

1 garlic clove, minced

½ teaspoon dried oregano, finely crumbled

¼ teaspoon dried thyme

⅛ teaspoon crushed hot red pepper

1 teaspoon cider vinegar or white wine vinegar

---

**1.** Rinse the okra and pat dry with paper towels. Trim a tiny slice off the stem, but do not cut into the pod of the okra. Put the okra in a bowl and toss with 1 tablespoon of the olive oil. Season the okra with the salt and black pepper.

**2.** Heat a grill pan over medium heat until hot enough to make a few drops of water sizzle. Put the okra on the hot pan, fitting them close together. Tent loosely with a sheet of aluminum foil and cook until flecked with brown grill marks on the bottom, 3 to 4 minutes. With tongs, turn the okra, cover again, and continue cooking until crisp-tender, about 3 minutes longer. Remove the okra to a plate.

**3.** In a small skillet, heat the remaining 2 tablespoons olive oil over medium heat. Add the garlic, oregano, thyme, and hot pepper. Cook, stirring, until the garlic and spices are aromatic, about 30 seconds. Remove the pan from the heat and stir in the vinegar. Drizzle the hot mixture over the okra. Serve warm or at room temperature.

# Grilled Red Bell Peppers, Onions, and Portobello Mushrooms

*For convenience, you can grill this trio of vegetables well ahead of time. Rewarm before serving or enjoy them at room temperature. These go well with any kind of meat, poultry, or fish as well as tossed with greens, pasta, or rice to make an unusual salad.*

*Makes 4 servings*

---

2 medium portobello mushrooms
2 tablespoons olive oil
2 tablespoons balsamic vinegar
1 teaspoon fresh lemon juice
½ teaspoon dried thyme

¼ teaspoon salt
2 large red bell peppers, quartered
    lengthwise and seeded
2 red onions, cut into thick rounds
⅛ teaspoon freshly ground pepper

---

**1.** Remove the stems from the mushrooms. With a melon-baller or small spoon, scoop out and discard the brown gills from the caps.

**2.** In a small bowl, whisk together the olive oil, vinegar, lemon juice, thyme, and salt. Brush some of the vinaigrette all over the mushrooms, bell peppers, and red onion rounds.

**3.** Heat a grill pan over medium heat until hot enough to make a few drops of water sizzle. Lay the vegetables on the hot pan, cover loosely with a sheet of aluminum foil, and cook, turning once or twice and brushing lightly with the remaining vinaigrette, until the peppers and onions are crisp-tender and the mushrooms are juicy and cooked through, 10 to 12 minutes.

**4.** Cut the peppers into strips and the mushrooms into slices. Leave the onion rounds intact. Season with black pepper and serve warm or at room temperature.

# Golden Plantain Coins

*Plantains are cooking bananas, which are very popular all over Mexico, the Caribbean, and Central America. They are available in most supermarkets. When ripe, plantains darken in color to almost black and yield to a slight pressure. Avoid plantains with any sign of mold on the skin. Grilled plantains are mildly sweet and absolutely delicious. They go especially well with grilled chicken and rice or black bean dishes. Try them for breakfast, drizzled with maple syrup.*

*Makes 4 servings*

---

2 ripe plantains
2 tablespoons vegetable oil

1 tablespoon melted butter
Salt

---

**1.** Cut the plantains in half crosswise and trim off the ends. Make a lengthwise cut through the tough skin and remove the peel. Cut the plantains crosswise into ¼-inch-thick rounds. Put the rounds in a medium bowl and toss with the oil and melted butter to coat.

**2.** Heat a grill pan over medium heat until hot enough to make a few drops of water sizzle. In batches if necessary, place the plantain rounds close together on the hot pan and sprinkle lightly with salt. Grill, turning 3 or 4 times, until tender and golden, with brown marks from the grill pan, about 5 minutes. Serve warm.

# Snappy Sugar Snap Peas

*Young, freshly picked sugar snap peas in their edible pods are a seasonal delight. The fact that they can be cooked so easily to al dente perfection on the grill pan may come as quite a surprise. Be sure to select small, firm peas that are plump and bright green. Sweet snap peas need little more than a dash of salt and a light drizzle of olive oil. I also like to dip them in soy sauce. Serve the peas as a side vegetable with any poultry, meat, or fish. Or serve them as an appetizer to be eaten with the fingers.*

*Makes 4 servings*

---

¾ pound small sugar snap peas
1 teaspoon olive oil

¼ teaspoon salt
⅓ cup soy sauce

---

**1.** Rinse the peas and pull off any strings. Put the peas in a pie plate. Add the olive oil and roll the pods in the oil. Season with the salt.

**2.** Heat a grill pan over medium heat until hot enough to make a few drops of water sizzle. Lay the snap peas close together on the pan and cover loosely with aluminum foil. Cook the peas for 3 minutes. They will be flecked with brown from the pan. Turn the peas over, cover with the foil, and cook 2 minutes longer.

**3.** Transfer the sugar snap peas to a bowl. Serve them warm or at room temperature. Pass the soy sauce on the side for dipping.

# Grilled Radicchio

*A relative newcomer for Americans, radicchio is a bitter red lettuce that comes to us from Italy. It has found a permanent place on the trendy vegetable scene for those who like its bite and beautiful deep color. Grilling mellows the vegetable slightly and turns it into an intriguing accent to accompany roasted, sautéed, or grilled meats.*

*Makes 4 servings*

---

2 small heads of radicchio (4 to 5 ounces each)
¼ cup extra-virgin olive oil

1½ teaspoons red wine vinegar
½ teaspoon salt
⅛ teaspoon freshly ground pepper

---

**1.** Remove any bruised outer leaves from the radicchio and cut the heads into quarters, leaving the cores attached. Brush the radicchio quarters with 1 tablespoon of the olive oil.

**2.** Heat a grill pan over medium heat until hot enough to make a few drops of water sizzle. Lay the radicchio on the hot pan and cook, turning 3 or 4 times, until the leaves are wilted and brown around the edges, about 5 minutes total. Remove to a platter.

**3.** Drizzle the remaining olive oil and the vinegar over the grilled radicchio. Season with the salt and pepper. Serve warm or at room temperature.

# Grilled Scallions

*Scallions, also called green onions in some parts of the country, are a terrific item to serve with steaks, burgers, pizzas, or as a part of just about any barbecue menu. Grilled scallions will stay slightly crunchy, and they are milder and sweeter than raw.*

*Makes 4 servings*

---

8 scallions, including the green tops
1 tablespoon olive oil

Salt and freshly ground pepper

---

**1.** Trim the tiny roots off the ends of the scallions, but do not cut into the white bulb. Rub the scallions all over with the olive oil. Season lightly with salt and pepper.
**2.** Heat a grill pan over medium heat until hot enough to make a few drops of water sizzle. Lay the scallions on the hot pan and cook, turning 3 or 4 times, until the scallions are marked with brown from the grill and the tops are limp and slightly charred, about 6 minutes. Serve the grilled scallions warm or at room temperature.

# Summer Squash Medley

*By "summer squash," I refer not just to the yellow crooknecks commonly referred to by that name, but to all the many varieties of tender squashes so abundant in summer: the yellow crooknecks as well as green and yellow zucchini and small yellow, pale green, and white pattypans. Choose whatever varieties you have in your garden or at your farmers' market.*

*Makes 4 servings*

---

4 small zucchini squash (about 4 inches long)

4 small yellow crookneck squash (about 4 inches long)

4 small pattypan squash (about 2 inches in diameter)

1 small garlic clove, crushed through a press

2 tablespoons olive oil

½ teaspoon salt

⅛ teaspoon freshly ground pepper

---

**1.** Cut all the squash in half lengthwise and put them in a large mixing bowl. Add the garlic and olive oil. Gently toss the squash to coat with oil. Season with the salt and pepper.

**2.** Heat a grill pan over medium heat until hot enough to make a few drops of water sizzle. Arrange the squash, cut sides down, on the pan, in batches if necessary, and cook until brown grill marks appear on the bottom, 4 to 5 minutes. Turn the squash over and cook until crisp-tender, about 5 minutes.

# Baby Sunburst Squash with Cheese Topping

*Summer squash come in a variety of shapes and colors, but I'm always drawn to the brilliant yellow scalloped sunburst squash. A simple cheese topping turns these little beauties into a great summer treat.*

*Makes 4 servings*

---

½ cup grated Swiss or cheddar cheese
1½ tablespoons fine bread crumbs
2 teaspoons mayonnaise
8 small yellow scalloped sunburst summer squash (about 2 inches in diameter)

2 tablespoons olive oil
½ teaspoon salt
¼ teaspoon freshly ground pepper

---

**1.** In a small bowl, combine the cheese, bread crumbs, and mayonnaise. Stir to mix well.

**2.** Preheat the oven broiler. With a sharp knife, trim about ¼ inch off the bottom of each squash, so that they will sit flat. Cut off the tops of the squash just above the scalloped edges to create a flat surface for the cheese topping. Brush the squash with the olive oil and season with the salt and pepper.

**3.** Heat a grill pan over medium heat until hot enough to make a few drops of water sizzle. Put the squash, cut sides down, on the heated pan and cook until brown grill marks appear, 3 to 4 minutes. Turn the squash over and cover with a sheet of aluminum foil. Cook until the squash is crisp-tender, about 5 minutes. Turn the squash 1 more time and cook for 2 minutes. Remove the squash to a baking sheet.

**4.** Put about 1 tablespoon of the cheese mixture on top of each squash. Broil about 4 inches from the heat until the topping is brown and crusty, 1 to 2 minutes. Serve hot or warm.

# Grilled Yams

*Sturdy root vegetables do exceptionally well on the grill, which brings out their natural sweetness. In place of yams, you could use the same technique to grill turnips or rutabagas or even parsnips—or a mix of winter vegetables. This goes especially well with chicken, ham, and pork.*

*Makes 4 servings*

---

2 pounds medium yams (choose long, narrow yams, rather than short, fat ones)

3 tablespoons olive oil

Salt and freshly ground pepper

---

**1.** Rinse and peel the yams. Cut them into ¼-inch-thick rounds and put them in a large mixing bowl. Toss with the olive oil to coat.

**2.** Heat a grill pan over medium-high heat until hot enough to make a few drops of water sizzle. Lay the vegetable rounds on the hot pan, in batches if necessary, and season lightly with salt and pepper. Cover loosely with a sheet of aluminum foil and cook until grill marks appear on the bottom of the rounds, 4 to 5 minutes. Turn the yams over and cover with the foil. Cook the second side until tender, 3 to 4 minutes longer. Serve hot.

## Chapter Seven

# Grilled Sandwiches, Tortillas, and Pizzas

There are so many possibilities in this category that you'll reach for the grill pan often to try some of the terrific recipes in this chapter. It's a pleasure every time you flip a sandwich or burrito to see the appetizing and distinctive grill marks that appear. The toasty flavor and crispy exterior of these foods will please everyone who likes fillings or toppings inside of, or on top of, bread or some other baked wrapping.

This chapter is filled with informal foods that are fun to eat for any casual occasion. You can grill just about anything you can put between slices of bread or roll up in tortillas or tuck inside pita breads, so use your imagination and try the grill pan for making the most of your own creations. You'll find inspiration among such recipes in this chapter as Chicken Quesadillas, Hot Chicken Croissant Sandwiches, Grilled Turkey Pita Pockets with Charmoula, even classic Reuben Sandwiches.

# Ground Turkey and Red Onion Burgers

*Ground turkey is very versatile, and these terrific grilled burgers are easy to make by using the equally versatile stove-top grill pan. Squares of aluminum foil keep the grilled onion rounds from falling apart while they cook. Toasting the cut sides of the buns enhances the toasty, lightly charred flavor of the sandwiches.*

*Makes 4 servings*

---

1 pound ground turkey meat
1 garlic clove, minced
2 tablespoons dry bread crumbs
2 tablespoons finely chopped fresh
   parsley
2 tablespoons milk (low-fat or skim
   milk is fine)
1 teaspoon Worcestershire sauce
½ teaspoon dried thyme leaves

½ teaspoon salt
¼ teaspoon freshly ground pepper
4 center cuts from a large red onion,
   sliced in ½-inch-thick rounds
2 tablespoons olive oil or vegetable oil
4 burger buns
Ketchup, mustard, mayonnaise, and
   lettuce

---

**1.** In a medium bowl, combine the ground turkey with the garlic, bread crumbs, parsley, milk, Worcestershire, thyme, ¼ teaspoon of the salt, and ⅛ teaspoon of the pepper. Blend well. Form the ground turkey into 4 equal-sized round patties about ½ inch thick and 4 inches in diameter. Put each onion round on a square of aluminum foil. Brush the turkey patties and the onions on both sides with oil. Season the onions with the remaining salt and pepper.

**2.** Heat the grill pan over medium heat until a few drops of water are hot enough to sizzle. Lay the turkey patties in the center of the pan and arrange the onion rounds on the foil squares near the outer edges. Cook the turkey burgers until brown grill marks appear, 4 to 5 minutes. Turn over and cook the second sides until no longer pink in the center, 2 to 3 minutes. Turn the onion rounds carefully 2 to 3 times with a small flexible spatula to keep them intact. The onions should be ready when the burgers are.

**3.** Remove the burgers and onions to a plate and cover to keep warm. Toast the buns, cut side down, for about 1 minute. Assemble the burgers by putting 1 patty and a portion of the onions on the bottom halves of the buns. Lay on the bun tops to form sandwiches. Pass ketchup, mustard, mayonnaise, and a plate of lettuce leaves at the table.

# Grilled Turkey Pita Pockets with Charmoula

*These sandwiches get their lively flavor from charmoula, a classic Moroccan sauce. Small, four-inch pitas are the perfect size for these sandwiches.*

*Makes 4 sandwiches*

---

½ cup parsley sprigs, loosely packed
½ cup cilantro leaves, loosely packed
2 garlic cloves, finely chopped
¼ cup extra-virgin olive oil
3 tablespoons fresh lemon juice
1 teaspoon red wine vinegar
1½ teaspoons Hungarian paprika
1½ teaspoons ground cumin

¼ teaspoon cayenne
¼ teaspoon salt
¼ teaspoon freshly ground pepper
4 turkey cutlets (4 to 5 ounces each)
4 (4-inch) pita breads
1 large tomato, thinly sliced
½ medium cucumber, thinly sliced

---

**1.** In a food processor or blender, combine the parsley, cilantro, garlic, olive oil, lemon juice, vinegar, paprika, cumin, cayenne, salt, and pepper. Puree until nearly smooth. Transfer the charmoula sauce to a bowl.

**2.** Heat a grill pan over medium heat until hot enough to make a few drops of water sizzle. Put the turkey cutlets on the hot pan and cook until brown grill marks appear on the bottom, 2 to 3 minutes. Turn the turkey over and cook the second side until the meat is no longer pink inside, about 2 minutes longer. Transfer the turkey to a carving board and cut into thin strips.

**3.** Slice off about one-third of each pita bread to open a pocket. Put the pitas on the heated grill pan and toast, turning, until the bread is soft and warm, about 1 minute. Stuff each pita with one-fourth of the turkey strips. Drizzle about 1 tablespoon of the sauce over each. Let each person add their own sliced tomato and cucumber.

---

# Hot Chicken Croissant Sandwiches

*Flaky, buttery croissants make sandwiches seem extra special. This hot version features grilled chicken breasts, melted Swiss cheese, and roasted peppers.*

*Makes 4 sandwiches*

---

¼ cup mayonnaise
2 tablespoons Dijon mustard
4 skinless, boneless chicken breast halves
2 teaspoons olive oil
½ teaspoon salt
¼ teaspoon freshly ground pepper

4 slices of Swiss cheese
4 croissants, split lengthwise
½ cup drained and coarsely chopped
    jarred roasted red peppers
Lettuce leaves

---

**1.** In a small bowl, blend the mayonnaise and mustard. Pound the chicken breasts between 2 sheets of plastic wrap with the flat side of a meat mallet or a rolling pin to an even thickness of ½ inch. Trim off any fat. Brush on both sides with the olive oil and season with the salt and pepper.

**2.** Heat a grill pan over medium heat until hot enough to make a few drops of water sizzle. Put the chicken breasts on the hot pan and cook until brown grill marks appear on the bottom, 3 to 4 minutes. Turn over and cook until the chicken is no longer pink inside, 3 to 4 minutes. Place 1 slice of cheese on top of each chicken breast and cook 1 minute longer, or until the cheese begins to melt.

**3.** Spread the mustard mayonnaise evenly over the 4 croissant bottoms. Spoon the chopped red peppers over the mayonnaise. Place 1 chicken breast with cheese on top of the peppers. Add lettuce leaves and cover with the croissant tops to make sandwiches.

# Philadelphia Cheese Steaks

*It's amazing that an American sandwich from the thirties, made with thinly sliced beefsteak, onions, and peppers, all fried in oil, piled on a soft French roll, and topped with melted cheese, continues in popularity today. This version, while not completely authentic, is quite delicious. Instead of being fried, the onions, peppers, and steaks are all cooked on the stove-top grill pan.*

*Makes 4 servings*

---

1 large sweet onion, such as Vidalia, thinly sliced

1 medium green bell pepper, thinly sliced

3 tablespoons vegetable oil

¾ teaspoon salt

½ teaspoon freshly ground pepper

1 pound minute steaks, thawed if frozen

4 French or Kaiser rolls, split in half

8 ounces shredded mozzarella or provolone cheese

---

**1.** In a medium bowl, toss the onion and bell pepper with 2 tablespoons of the oil to coat lightly. Season with ¼ teaspoon of the salt and ⅛ teaspoon of the pepper. Brush the steaks with the remaining 1 tablespoon of oil. Season with the remaining salt and pepper.

**2.** Heat a grill pan over medium heat until hot enough to make a few drops of water sizzle. Put the onions and pepper strips on the hot pan and cook, turning and tossing with tongs, until lightly browned and fairly tender, 4 to 5 minutes. Transfer to a plate.

**3.** Put the minute steaks on the same hot pan, in batches if necessary, so they form a single layer, and cook, turning, until just cooked through and barely marked from the grill, about 30 to 60 seconds per side.

**4.** Preheat the oven broiler. On a baking sheet, lay out the 4 bottom roll halves. Divide the grilled steaks among the buns, piling up the meat as needed. Cover with the grilled onions and peppers. Top with the cheese. Broil about 4 inches from the heat until the cheese melts, 1 to 2 minutes. Put on the roll tops and serve while hot.

# Green Chile Cheeseburgers

*Makes 4 servings*

1 pound lean ground beef
1 teaspoon chili powder
1 teaspoon salt
2 teaspoons olive oil
4 slices of cheddar cheese

2 tablespoons mayonnaise
2 tablespoons ketchup
4 onion rolls
1 (4-ounce) can whole green chiles,
   rinsed, seeded, and cut into strips
   ½ inch wide

**1.** In a medium bowl, gently mix the ground beef, chili powder, and salt. Form into 4 patties about ½ inch thick. Brush the patties lightly with the olive oil.

**2.** Heat a grill pan over medium heat until hot enough to make a few drops of water sizzle. Put the patties on the hot pan and cook until brown and marked from the grill on the bottom, 4 to 5 minutes. Turn the patties over and cook until brown on the second side and barely pink on the inside, another 2 to 3 minutes. Put 1 slice of cheese on top of each. Remove the burgers to a plate.

**2.** Open the rolls and toast on the grill pan, cut sides down, until lightly browned, 1 to 2 minutes. Spread the mayonnaise and ketchup equally among the toasted rolls. Cover the bottom half of each bun with the green chile strips, add the cheeseburgers, and sandwich with the tops of the buns.

# Fresh Salmon Burgers

*Makes 6 servings*

---

1 pound salmon fillet, skinned and
  coarsely chopped
¾ cup mayonnaise
½ cup fine dry bread crumbs
2 scallions, finely chopped
1 tablespoon chopped fresh dill or
  parsley
1 tablespoon fresh lemon juice

1 teaspoon Dijon mustard
¼ teaspoon salt
Dash of cayenne
2 tablespoons melted butter
12 slices of whole wheat bread, toasted
6 tomato slices
6 lettuce leaves

---

**1.** In a medium bowl, combine the salmon, ¼ cup of the mayonnaise, the bread crumbs, scallions, dill, lemon juice, mustard, salt, and cayenne. Form into 6 patties about ½ inch thick.

**2.** Coat a grill pan with nonstick cooking spray, then heat over medium heat until hot enough to make a few drops of water sizzle. Brush the patties with the melted butter and put them on the hot pan. Cook, turning, until brown and crusty on both sides, about 6 minutes total. Remove the salmon burgers to a plate.

**3.** To assemble, put 1 slice of toast on each of 6 plates. Spread about 2 teaspoons of the remaining mayonnaise on each slice of toast. Layer each with a salmon burger, tomato, and lettuce. Spread the remaining 6 slices of toast generously with the remaining mayonnaise and sandwich on top.

# Goat Cheese Finger Sandwiches

*These unique grilled triangle sandwiches make a marvelous snack or cocktail-party hors d'oeuvre.*

*Makes 4 servings*

---

5 ounces soft fresh white goat cheese, at room temperature

1 scallion, finely chopped

2 tablespoons finely chopped kalamata or other black olives

1 tablespoon finely chopped fresh oregano or ½ teaspoon dried

¼ teaspoon salt

⅛ teaspoon freshly ground pepper

8 slices of egg bread or thinly sliced firm-textured white sandwich bread

¼ cup chopped oil-packed sun-dried tomatoes, drained

2 tablespoons unsalted butter, at room temperature

---

**1.** In a medium bowl, combine the goat cheese, scallion, olives, oregano, salt, and pepper. Lay the 8 bread slices on a flat surface. Spread the cheese evenly over the bread. Top 4 of the slices with 1 tablespoon of the sun-dried tomatoes. Invert the remaining 4 bread slices to make sandwiches. Butter the outside of the sandwiches on both sides.

**2.** Heat the grill pan over medium heat until a few drops of water are hot enough to sizzle. Put the sandwiches on the hot pan and cook, turning once, until the cheese is melted and the sandwiches are toasted and marked from the grill, 1 to 2 minutes on each side.

**3.** Cut the sandwiches diagonally into quarters. Serve warm.

# Portobello, Onion, and Roquefort Open-Face Sandwiches

*A meatless stacked sandwich built on hearty country bread makes a satisfying meal.*

*Makes 4 servings*

---

4 slices of country sourdough bread, cut about ¾ inch thick
3 tablespoons olive oil
4 portobello mushroom caps, about 3 inches in diameter
2 medium onions, sliced about ½ inch thick

½ teaspoon salt
¼ teaspoon freshly ground pepper
¼ cup crumbled Roquefort cheese
2 tablespoons mayonnaise
Lettuce leaves
2 medium tomatoes, sliced

---

**1.** Brush the bread slices on both sides with 1 tablespoon of the olive oil. Remove the mushroom stems and scoop out the black gills from the caps. Brush the mushrooms and the onions with the remaining 2 tablespoons of oil and season with the salt and pepper.

**2.** Heat a grill pan over medium heat until hot enough to make a few drops of water sizzle. In batches if necessary, put the mushrooms and onions on the hot pan. Cover loosely with a sheet of aluminum and cook until brown on both sides, about 4 minutes per side. Remove the mushrooms to a cutting board and cut crosswise into ½-inch-thick slices. Separate the onions into rings.

**3.** Toast the bread until light brown on both sides. Combine the cheese and mayonnaise and spread equally over each bread slice. Put lettuce leaves on each bread slice and top each toast equally with tomatoes, mushrooms, and onions. Serve immediately.

# Red Onion, Cheddar Cheese, and Tomato Sandwiches

*For extra interest and extra flavor from a traditional grilled cheese sandwich, add grilled onions and vine-ripened tomatoes. Select an oat and whole grain bread, and you've got something doubly special.*

*Makes 4 servings*

---

1 large red onion, sliced into rounds about ⅜ inch thick
1 tablespoon olive oil
Salt and freshly ground pepper
8 large slices of bread

2 tablespoons mayonnaise
8 tomato slices
8 slices of sharp cheddar cheese, about ¼ inch thick

---

**1.** Brush the onion with the olive oil. Season lightly with salt and pepper. Heat a grill pan over medium heat until hot enough to make a few drops of water sizzle. Put the onion rounds on the hot pan and cook, turning 3 or 4 times, until browned and crisp-tender, 3 to 4 minutes. Remove the onion rounds to a plate and separate into rings.

**2.** Lay the bread slices on a flat surface. Spread the mayonnaise over 4 slices. Divide the grilled onion rings among the 4 bread slices. Top each with 2 tomato and 2 cheese slices. Close the sandwiches with the remaining 4 bread slices.

**3.** Reheat the grill pan as before. Lay the sandwiches on the hot pan and toast, turning, until brown grill marks appear on both sides and the cheese is melted, 2 to 3 minutes per side. Serve while hot.

# Beefsteak Sandwiches with Refried Beans and Sizzled Onions

*These sandwiches are a whole meal on a bun. Serve tortilla chips on the side.*

*Makes 4 servings*

---

3 tablespoons olive oil
1 large onion, thinly sliced
1 teaspoon Worcestershire sauce
Salt and freshly ground pepper
4 (6- to 8-ounce) boneless beef rib steaks, about ½ inch thick, trimmed of excess fat

3 tablespoons mayonnaise or softened butter
4 soft French sandwich rolls, halved lengthwise
1 cup canned refried beans, heated
Ketchup or prepared red salsa

---

**1.** In a large skillet, heat 2 tablespoons of the olive oil over medium-high heat. Add the onion and cook, stirring occasionally, until the onion is golden brown, 4 to 5 minutes. Remove the pan from the heat, add the Worcestershire, and toss. Season lightly with salt and pepper.

**2.** Brush the steaks with the remaining 1 tablespoon olive oil and season generously with salt and pepper. Heat a grill pan over medium heat until hot enough to make a few drops of water sizzle. Put the steaks on the hot pan and cook until brown grill marks appear on the bottom, 4 to 5 minutes. Turn the steaks over and cook until brown on the outside and pink inside, 3 to 4 minutes, or longer to the desired degree of doneness. Remove the steaks to a cutting board and let stand about 5 minutes. Slice the steaks crosswise into strips ½ inch thick.

**3.** Spread the mayonnaise or butter on both cut sides of the rolls. Spoon about 3 tablespoons of the warm refried beans onto each roll. Top with the steak strips and browned onion. Add ketchup or salsa to taste, close the sandwiches, and serve.

# Reuben Sandwiches

*A Reuben is a hefty American creation. This toasted version joins corned beef, Swiss cheese, sauerkraut, and Russian dressing with rye bread and crunchy dill pickles on the side.*

*Makes 4 sandwiches*

---

8 slices of Russian or Jewish rye bread
½ pound thinly sliced deli corned beef
1½ cups well-drained sauerkraut, at
   room temperature
¼ cup mayonnaise
2 tablespoons chili sauce

1 tablespoon pickle relish
8 slices of Swiss cheese
1½ to 2 tablespoons butter, at room
   temperature
Sliced dill pickles

---

**1.** Lay out 4 bread slices on a flat surface. Put one-fourth of the corned beef on each of the slices. In a medium bowl, mix the sauerkraut, mayonnaise, chili sauce, and relish. Pile on top of the corned beef. Put 2 slices of cheese on top of each and cover with the remaining 4 bread slices to form sandwiches. Butter the outsides of the sandwiches.

**2.** Heat a grill pan over medium heat until hot enough to make a few drops of water sizzle. Lay the sandwiches on the heated pan and toast, turning once, until brown grill marks appear on both sides of the sandwiches and the cheese is melted, 4 to 6 minutes total. Cut each sandwich in half diagonally and serve hot with sliced dill pickles on the side.

# Texas Barbecued Pork Sandwiches

*Thin slices of grilled pork loin are slathered with a robust barbecue sauce to make hefty barbecued pork sandwiches.*

*Makes 4 sandwiches*

---

| | |
|---|---|
| 1 pound thinly sliced boneless pork loin | 1 cup chili sauce |
| 2 tablespoons vegetable oil | 1½ tablespoons brown sugar |
| Salt and freshly ground pepper | 2 teaspoons red wine vinegar |
| 4 sesame burger buns, split | 1 teaspoon Worcestershire sauce |
| 1 medium onion, thinly sliced | 1 teaspoon Dijon mustard |
| 2 garlic cloves, minced | 1⅓ cups finely shredded cabbage |

---

**1.** Pound the pork slices lightly to flatten to an even thickness. Brush the pork with 1 tablespoon of the oil and season lightly with salt and pepper.

**2.** Coat a grill pan with nonstick cooking spray, then heat over medium heat until hot enough to make a few drops of water sizzle. Put the meat on the hot pan and cook, turning 2 to 3 times, until nicely browned and cooked through, 3 to 4 minutes. Remove the meat to a plate. Toast the sesame buns on the hot grill pan, cut sides down, until grill marks appear, about 2 minutes. Move the buns to the coolest part of the pan and turn off the heat.

**3.** In a medium saucepan, heat the remaining oil over medium heat. Add the onion and garlic. Cook, stirring, until the onion begins to brown, 3 to 4 minutes. Add the chili sauce, brown sugar, vinegar, Worcestershire, and mustard. Bring to a boil, reduce the heat to low, and simmer, uncovered, for 5 minutes.

**4.** Add the grilled pork slices and any juices that have accumulated on the plate and heat through. To serve, pile the pork and sauce on the bottom halves of the toasted rolls. Top each with ⅓ cup shredded cabbage and cover with the roll tops.

# Toasted Ham and Cheese on Dark Rye Bread

*Try making one of my favorite toasted sandwiches on the grill pan. Accompany with pickles, tomato wedges, and a bowl of potato salad or potato chips for a complete lunch.*

*Makes 4 servings*

---

8 slices of dark rye bread
2 tablespoons mayonnaise
4 teaspoons mustard of your choice
4 slices of Swiss or cheddar cheese

4 slices of fully cooked deli ham, such
    as Black Forest or honey baked
2 tablespoons butter, at room
    temperature

---

**1.** Lay out the 8 bread slices on a working surface. Spread the mayonnaise on the surface of 4 slices. Spread the mustard on the remaining 4 slices. Put the cheese slices on the mayonnaise and top with the ham. Turn the 4 bread slices with mustard over and lay on top of the ham to form sandwiches. Spread the tops of the sandwiches with half the butter.

**2.** Heat a grill pan over medium heat until hot enough to make a few drops of water sizzle. Lay the sandwiches, buttered sides down, on the hot pan. Toast until the bottoms are brown and crusty, 2 to 3 minutes. Butter the tops and turn the sandwiches over. Toast until the second sides are brown and the cheese is melted, 1 to 2 minutes. Remove from the pan, cut in half, and serve while hot.

# Breakfast Turkey Sausage Burritos

*Packaged fresh turkey sausage links are available in the meat section of most supermarkets. The lean little links cook to an appetizing brown on the grill pan. Enjoy these sausage burritos for breakfast or a quick satisfying snack any time.*

*Makes 4 servings*

---

8 fresh turkey breakfast sausage links
   (packaged 14 per container)
1 cup canned refried beans

4 (7-inch) flour tortillas
½ cup bottled salsa
½ cup shredded cheddar cheese

---

**1.** Heat a grill pan over medium heat until hot enough to make a few drops of water sizzle. Put the sausages on the hot pan and cook, turning, until lightly browned and no longer pink in the center, 12 to 15 minutes. Remove the sausages to a cutting board, chop coarsely, and put into a medium bowl. Add the refried beans and stir to mix with the sausages.

**2.** Reheat the grill pan over medium heat and warm the tortillas on the pan, turning until they are soft and pliable, 1 to 2 minutes per tortilla. Lay the tortillas on a flat surface. Spread one-fourth of the sausage and bean mixture over each tortilla. Top with 2 tablespoons each salsa and cheese.

**3.** Roll the bottom of the tortillas up over the filling, fold in the sides, and roll up like an egg roll. Put the burritos on the heated grill pan. Cook, turning, until the burritos are heated through and the cheese is melted, 3 to 4 minutes. Serve hot.

# Chicken Quesadillas

*Double your pleasure by filling flour tortillas with both chicken and cheese for a zesty snack or light meal. The grill pan does double duty by first cooking the chicken and then crisping up the filled quesadillas just before serving.*

*Makes 4 servings*

---

3 skinless, boneless chicken breast halves

About 1½ tablespoons vegetable oil

½ teaspoon salt

2 scallions, chopped

½ cup thick and chunky salsa

8 (7- to 8-inch) flour tortillas

1 cup shredded Monterey Jack cheese (about 4 ounces)

¼ cup sour cream

Chopped cilantro

---

**1.** Place the chicken breasts between 2 sheets of plastic wrap and pound gently to an even thickness of ½ inch. Brush the chicken with some of the oil to coat lightly and season with the salt.

**2.** Heat a grill pan over medium heat until hot enough to make a few drops of water sizzle. Lay the chicken on the hot pan and cook until brown grill marks appear on the bottom, 5 to 6 minutes. Turn and cook until the second side is light brown and the chicken is white throughout but still juicy, 3 to 4 minutes. Transfer the chicken to a carving board and cut the chicken into ¼-inch strips. Put the chicken strips in a medium bowl. Add the scallions and salsa and stir to mix.

**3.** To assemble the quesadillas, place 4 of the tortillas on a flat surface. Divide the chicken mixture equally among the tortillas and top each with about 2 tablespoons cheese. Top with the remaining 4 tortillas. Brush the tops with vegetable oil.

**4.** Heat the grill pan over medium heat as before. One at a time, invert the quesadillas onto the hot pan, oiled sides down and cook until lightly browned on the bottom,

---

3 to 4 minutes. Brush the tops with oil, carefully lift with a wide spatula, and turn over. Cook until the second side is lightly browned and the cheese is melted, 2 to 3 minutes. To serve, cut each quesadilla into quarters. Garnish with a tablespoon of sour cream and a sprinkling of chopped cilantro.

# Party Quesadillas

*Layers of grilled chicken, green chiles, cheese, and black olives mixed with sour cream and salsa can, of course, be enjoyed any time, but they are so popular, I find that, cut into wedges, they make great party nibbles.*

*Makes 4 servings*

---

4 skinless, boneless chicken breast halves, cut crosswise into ½-inch strips
4 to 5 teaspoons vegetable oil
½ teaspoon salt
¼ teaspoon freshly ground pepper
1 cup shredded Monterey Jack cheese (about 4 ounces)

1 (7-ounce) can diced green chiles
1 (4-ounce) can chopped black olives
½ cup sour cream
2 scallions, thinly sliced
8 (8- or 9-inch) flour tortillas
½ cup thick and chunky red salsa

---

**1.** Brush the chicken breast strips with 2 teaspoons of the vegetable oil and season with the salt and pepper. Heat a grill pan over medium heat until hot enough to make a few drops of water sizzle. Put the chicken on the heated pan and cook, turning with tongs, until the strips are flecked with brown from the grill and the meat is white inside, 3 to 4 minutes. Remove the chicken to a cutting board and chop coarsely.

**2.** In a medium bowl, combine the cheese, chiles, olives, sour cream, and scallions. Lay out 4 of the tortillas on a flat surface. Spread the cheese mixture equally over each tortilla, leaving a ½-inch margin around the edges. Scatter the chopped chicken over the cheese mixture. Spoon 2 tablespoons salsa over each. Top with the remaining 4 tortillas and press the edges together gently.

**3.** Brush the tops of the tortillas with some of the remaining oil. Heat the grill pan again over medium heat. Invert 1 quesadilla onto the heated pan. Press the edges together to make contact with the pan. Cook until the bottom tortilla is marked with brown grill marks and crisp, about 2 minutes. Brush the top with oil and carefully turn over with a wide spatula. Cook the second side until crisp, 1 to 2 minutes longer. Remove to a cutting board and cut into quarters. Repeat with the remaining quesadillas. Serve warm.

# Vegetarian Tortilla Turnovers

*Makes 4 servings*

---

4 (9-inch) flour tortillas
4 ounces mild white goat cheese
1 (4-ounce) jar roasted red peppers,
    drained and chopped

1 (6-ounce) jar marinated artichoke
    hearts, drained and chopped
¼ cup thick and chunky red salsa
4 teaspoons vegetable oil

---

**1.** Heat a grill pan over medium heat until hot enough to make a few drops of water sizzle. One or two at a time, lay the tortillas on the grill and cook, turning once, until warm and flexible, 1 to 2 minutes. Wrap the warm tortillas stacked, in a clean tea towel. Remove the grill from the heat.

**2.** Spread one-fourth of the goat cheese over 1 tortilla. Layer one-fourth each of the roasted peppers, artichokes, and salsa on half of each tortilla. Fold the tortilla over to enclose the filling. Transfer to a baking sheet. Repeat with the remaining tortillas and filling. Brush both sides of the turnovers lightly with oil.

**3.** Reheat the grill pan. Put the turnovers on the hot pan and cook, turning, until brown grill marks appear on both sides and the turnovers are heated through, 3 to 4 minutes total. Cut the turnovers in half and serve warm.

# Pepperoni Pizza

*The stove-top grill pan makes a fine grilled pizza—right in your kitchen. For simplicity, use refrigerated or frozen pizza or bread dough from the supermarket.*

*Makes 4 individual pizzas*

---

1 (10-ounce) package refrigerated pizza dough

1 tablespoon olive oil

1 cup prepared marinara or pizza sauce

8 ounces shredded mozzarella

12 ounces thinly sliced pepperoni

½ cup freshly grated Parmesan cheese

---

**1.** Remove dough from package. Cut into 4 equal pieces. Roll each piece into a ball and flatten into a disk shape. Cover the dough and let rest 20 minutes at room temperature for easier handling. On a lightly floured board, roll out one disk to a 5- or 6-inch circle. Use the tips of your fingers to assist in pushing and shaping the dough. Brush one-fourth of the olive oil lightly over the dough and let rest 5 to 6 minutes.

**2.** Meanwhile, put the marinara sauce, shredded mozzarella, pepperoni, and Parmesan cheese in separate bowls and set near the stove. Heat a grill pan over medium heat until hot enough to make a few drops of water sizzle. Lay one disk of pizza dough on the pan and cook until lightly puffed and with grill marks stamped on the bottom, 2 to 3 minutes.

**3.** Turn the crust over and immediately cover with ¼ cup of the marinara sauce. Sprinkle about ½ cup of the mozzarella cheese over the sauce. Arrange one-fourth of the pepperoni slices on top and sprinkle 2 tablespoons of Parmesan cheese over the pizza. Tent loosely with a sheet of aluminum foil and cook, rotating the pizza once or twice, until the topping is hot, the cheese is melted, and the bottom is brown and crusty, 3 to 5 minutes. Remove the pizza to a board, cut into wedges, and serve. Repeat with the remaining dough and toppings to make 3 more pizzas.

# Grilled Pizza with Artichoke Hearts and Black Olives

*It's great fun to turn out stove-top pizzas whenever the mood strikes. Prepared refrigerated pizza dough from the supermarket makes the process possible in a short time. The cold dough is quite resistant and must be brought to room temperature before shaping. After a rest period, it will become quite easy to handle. The entire grilling time is less than 10 minutes.*

*Makes 4 individual pizzas*

---

1 (10-ounce) package refrigerated pizza
    dough
4 teaspoons olive oil
1 cup prepared pizza sauce
1 (6-ounce) jar marinated artichoke
    hearts, drained and chopped

1 (4-ounce) can chopped black olives
3 scallions, finely chopped
½ cup freshly grated Parmesan cheese

---

**1.** Remove the dough from the package. Cut into 4 equal pieces. Roll into balls and flatten into disks. Cover and let rest 20 minutes at room temperature. On a lightly floured board, roll out one disk to a 5- or 6-inch circle. Use the tips of your fingers to assist in pushing and shaping the dough. Brush with 1 teaspoon of the olive oil and let stand about 5 minutes.

**2.** Meanwhile, put the pizza sauce in a small bowl. In a medium bowl, mix together the artichokes, olives, and scallions. Put the cheese in another small bowl. Set the toppings near the stove.

**3.** Heat a grill pan over medium heat until hot enough to make a few drops of water sizzle. Lay the rolled pizza on the hot pan and cook until lightly puffed with grill marks stamped on the bottom, 2 to 3 minutes. Turn the pizza over and immediately spread with ¼ cup of the pizza sauce. Spoon one-fourth of the artichoke mixture over the sauce and top with 2 tablespoons Parmesan cheese. Cover the pizza loosely with foil and cook, rotating the pizza once or twice, until the topping is hot and the bottom is brown and crusty, 3 to 5 minutes. Remove to a carving board, cut into wedges, and serve. Repeat with the remaining dough and toppings to make 3 more pizzas.

# *Index*

Bread. *See also* Pita; Toast(s)
  bruschetta with red bell pepper, scallions, and feta cheese, 9
Breakfast turkey sausage burritos, 199
Brie, corn tortilla quesadillas with jalapeños and, 13
Bruschetta with red bell pepper, scallions, and feta cheese, 9
Burgers
  cheeseburgers, green chile, 190
  fresh salmon, 191
  ground turkey and red onion, 184
Burritos, breakfast turkey sausage, 199
Butter
  ginger, grilled halibut with, 80
  lemon
    and capers, fillet of sole with, 90
    grilled mussels with, 99
  lemon, Belgian endive with, 166
  lime parsley, snapper fillets with, 87
  mustard, asparagus with, 165
Butterflied leg of lamb, 162

Cabbage
  -carrot slaw, grilled shrimp with, 54
  chicken, and kidney bean salad, with Gorgonzola cheese, 66
  wedges, crunchy grilled, 167
Caesar salad, grilled chicken, 70
Cajun hot chicken salad, 62
Calamari steaks, speedy, 98
Calf's liver with onion and green pepper, grilled, 129
California shrimp toasts, 26
Canadian bacon and potato salad, 76
Caper(s)
  fillet of sole with lemon butter and, 90
  tomato, and olive relish, swordfish with, 91
Carrot(s)
  -cabbage slaw, grilled shrimp with, 54
  with cumin, pan-roasted, 170
Cashews, roasted, sweet-and-sour grilled chicken with, 112
Catalan tomato toast, 10
Catfish, grilled, with zesty tartar sauce, 79
Cauliflower
  with Asiago cream sauce and ham, 168
  salad, pan-grilled, with red onion vinaigrette, 77
  salad with Oregon hazelnut dressing, 44
Char-grilled chicken with Asian noodle salad, 64
Charmoula, grilled turkey pita pockets with, 186
Cheddar cheese
  in green chile cheeseburgers, 190
  red onion, and tomato sandwiches, 194
  and salsa quesadillas, 11

Cheese
  Brie, corn tortilla quesadillas with jalapeños and, 13
  Cheddar
    in green chile cheeseburgers, 190
    red onion, and tomato sandwiches, 194
    and salsa quesadillas, 11
  feta
    bruschetta with red bell pepper, scallions, and, 9
    chicken breasts stuffed with olives, sun-dried tomatoes, and, 142
    grilled eggplant salad with tomato, basil, and, 45
  goat
    finger sandwiches, 192
    toasted pita wedges with herbed, 17
    in vegetarian tortilla turnovers, 204
  Gorgonzola, chicken, kidney bean, and cabbage salad with, 66
  Monterey Jack
    in chicken quesadillas, 205
    in crab quesadillas, 21
    in party quesadillas, 207
    and salsa quesadillas, 11
    in zucchini, jalapeño, and cheese quesadillas, 12
  quesadillas
    and salsa, 11
    chicken, 200
    corn tortilla, with Brie and jalapeños, 13
    crab, 21
    party, 202
    zucchini, jalapeño, and, 12
  Roquefort
    dressing, portobello mushroom, zucchini, and onion salad with, 50
    open-face sandwiches, portobello, onion, and, 193
  steaks, Philadelphia, 188
  Swiss
    in Reuben sandwiches, 196
    toasted ham and, on dark rye bread, 198
  topping, baby sunburst squash with, 181
Cheeseburgers, green chile, 190
Chicken
  breasts
    with Italian salsa verde, 111
    with Mexican red chili-citrus sauce, 108
    with orange-thyme sauce, 104
    in party quesadillas, 202
    stuffed with feta cheese, olives, and sun-dried tomatoes, 142
    with tomato-wine sauce, 146
  croissant sandwiches, hot, 187
  garlic, grilled, with couscous, pecans, and raisins, 106

with tuna stuffing, grilled, 27
turkey patties, 116
poblano, grilled beef steak, tomatoes, and, over pasta, 126
sweet bell
    green, grilled calf's liver with onion and, 129
    lamb steaks with onions and, 135
    red. *See* Red bell pepper(s)
Pepperoni pizza, 205
Philadelphia cheese steaks, 188
Pickled red onions, 122
    tequila-lime flank steak with, 120
Pineapple
    salsa, mahimahi with, 83
    shrimp, sweet-and-sour, 101
Pine nuts, toasted, tuna steaks with sun-dried tomatoes and,
        93
Pita
    pockets, grilled turkey, with charmoula, 186
    triangles with hummus, toasted, 16
    wedges with herbed goat cheese, toasted, 17
Pizza
    with artichoke hearts and black olives, grilled, 206
    pepperoni, 205
Plantain(s)
    Bahama Mama snapper fillets with, 88
    coins, golden, 176
Poblano peppers, grilled beef steak, tomatoes, and, over pasta,
        126
Polish kielbasa sausage snacks, 36
Pork
    chicken, and apple sausage patties, 114
    chops, mustard-seasoned, 130
    roast with Szechuan chile sauce, 154
    sandwiches, Texas barbecued, 197
    and scallions, Korean spicy grilled, 131
    tenderloin
        with onion and mustard cream sauce, 156
        with red pepper relish, 158
        roasted, with spiced chili rub, 159
    tortilla wraps with avocado salsa, grilled, 34
Portobello mushroom(s)
    grilled red bell peppers, onions, and, 175
    onion, and Roquefort open-face sandwiches, 193
    zucchini, and onion salad with Roquefort dressing, 50
Potato salad, Canadian bacon and, 76

Quesadillas
    cheese and salsa, 11
    chicken, 200
    corn tortilla, with Brie and jalapeños, 13
    crab, 21

party, 202
zucchini, jalapeño, and cheese, 12

Radicchio, grilled, 178
Ragout, mushroom, grilled corn cakes with, 14
Rainbow trout, grilled Idaho, with toasted almonds, 92
Raisins, grilled garlic chicken with couscous, pecans, and, 106
Red bell pepper(s)
    bruschetta with scallions, feta cheese, and, 9
    onions, and portobello mushrooms, grilled, 175
    roasted
        relish, pork tenderloin with, 158
        sauce, tiger shrimp with sweet, 102
        in vegetarian tortilla turnovers, 204
    salad
        corn, black bean, and, grilled, 42
        fennel, mushroom, and, 46
    sauce, seared scallops with corn and sweet, 94
Red onions. *See* Onion(s), red
Refried beans
    in breakfast turkey sausage burritos, 199
    and sizzled onions, beefsteak sandwiches with, 195
Relish
    red pepper, pork tenderloin with, 158
    tomato, olive, and caper, swordfish with, 91
    tomato-mint, lamb patties with, 139
Reuben sandwiches, 196
Roasted pork tenderloin with spiced chili rub, 159
Romesco sauce, grilled shrimp with, 24
Roquefort
    dressing, portobello mushroom, zucchini, and onion salad
        with, 50
    open-face sandwiches, portobello, onion, and, 193
Rosemary tuna brochettes with toasted garlic mayonnaise, 28

Saffron, snapper fillets with, 89
Salad(s), 39–77
    Asian noodle, char-grilled chicken with, 64
    asparagus, with orange and black olive dressing, 40
    beef, Mexican grilled, 74
    beef patty taco, 72
    Canadian bacon and potato, 76
    cauliflower, pan-grilled, with red onion vinaigrette, 77
    cauliflower, with Oregon hazelnut dressing, 44
    chicken
        Caesar, grilled, 70
        Cajun hot, 62
        kidney bean, cabbage, and, with Gorgonzola cheese, 66
        spinach and, with apples and chutney dressing, 68
    chopped vegetable, with grilled fennel, 52
    corn, red bell pepper, and black bean, grilled, 42